THE BEACH

I came up in the water and I still had my rifle, my pack and my map case. I tore free of my gas mask.

I caught a flash of amtracs burning in one long line. I couldn't see Buck or anyone near me in the water. There must have been hundreds there; but my mind played some kind of strange trick and I saw no one and thought I was alone.

I began to slog in. Underwater, the beach was potted and full of holes. I stepped in deep places and fell more than once. But I don't remember seeing anyone. Around and above and everywhere the air hummed and sang. The zip, zip, zip became so steady it settled into one drone at high pitch. I ran into the humming smoke, floundering sometimes, but running on.

I fell out of the water and on to the beach. The sand was gray and rough and littered with splintered palm trees and chunks of coral. For the first time I saw men around me. Later I learned that some of my closest and best friends died in the water off Beach White 2 in Peleliu. But I never saw them. I ran around them or stepped over them, and there was one great anxiety—where was Buck? I had run through some of the fiercest fire put down on any landing beach in the war, and flopped down on the shore, I lay catching my breath and worrying about Buck. I was on the beach, but I had no idea what to do next.

THE BANTAM WAR BOOK SERIES

This series of books is about a world on fire.

The carefully chosen volumes in the Bantam War Book Series cover the full dramatic sweep of World War II. Many are eyewitness accounts by the men who fought in a global conflict as the world's future hung in the balance. Fighter pilots, tank commanders and infantry captains, among many others, recount exploits of individual courage. They present vivid portraits of brave men, true stories of gallantry, moving sagas of survival and stark tragedies of untimely death.

In 1933 Nazi Germany marched to become an empire that was to last a thousand years. In only twelve years that empire was destroyed, and ever since, the country has been bisected by her conquerors. Italy relinquished her colonial lands, as did Japan. These were the losers. The winners also lost the empires they had so painfully seized over the centuries. And one, Russia, lost over twenty million dead.

Those wartime 1940s were a simple, even a hopeful time. Hats came in only two colors, white and black, and after an initial battering the Allied nations started on a long laborious march toward victory. It was a time when sane men believed the world would evolve into a decent place, but, as with all futures, there was no one then who could really forecast the world that we know now.

There are many ways to think about war. It has always been hard to understand the motivations and braveries of Axis soldiers fighting to enslave and dominate their neighbors. Yet is is impossible to know the hammer without the anvil, and to comprehend ourselves we must know the people we once fought against.

Through these books we can discover what it was like to take part in the war that was a final experience for nearly fifty million human beings. In so doing we may discover the strength to make a world as good as the one contained in those dreams and aspirations once believed by heroic men. We must understand our past as an honor to those dead who can no longer choose. They exchanged their lives in a hope for this future that we now inhabit. Though the fight took place many years ago, each of us remains as a living part of it.

MARINE AT WAR

RUSSELL DAVIS

BANTAM BOOKS
TORONTO • NEW YORK • LONDON • SYDNEY • AUCKLAND

*This edition contains the complete text
of the original hardcover edition.*
NOT ONE WORD HAS BEEN OMITTED

MARINE AT WAR
*A Bantam Book / published by arrangement with
the authors*

PRINTING HISTORY
Little Brown edition published in 1961
Bantam edition / June 1988

Illustrations by Greg Beecham.

Maps by Alan McKnight.

ISBN 0-553-27117-2

Published simultaneously in the United States and Canada

Bantam Books are published by Bantam Books, a division of
Bantam Doubleday Dell Publishing Group, Inc. Its trademark,
consisting of the words "Bantam Books" and the portrayal of a
rooster, is Registered in U.S. Patent and Trademark Office and
in other countries. Marca Registrada. Bantam Books, 666 Fifth
Avenue, New York, New York 10103.

PRINTED IN THE UNITED STATES OF AMERICA

O   0 9 8 7 6 5 4 3 2 1

To my sons:
Chris, Jeff, Tim and Rusty

We would like to express our thanks to the U.S. Marine Corps for giving us permission to quote the passage in the final chapter which is taken from *The Old Breed: A History of the First Marine Division in World War II*.

CONTENTS

FOREWORD

I'm no expert in war. My service was in the Second Battalion of the First Marine Regiment from April of 1944 until February of 1946. My jobs were Combat Intelligence scout, rifleman, plans and operations sergeant, and rifle squad leader. As a Marine infantryman I was no better than average. I served through two major campaigns, Peleliu and Okinawa, and I was under fire in a few other patrol actions. I was wounded twice, cited for bravery once, and two times I was too frightened to do the job to which I was assigned.

My sons have asked me many questions about war. I have always tried to answer their questions, but sometimes the answers weren't true, and sometimes they weren't complete. It takes time to think out a good and true answer. It is very hard for a father not to make himself seem braver and wiser to his sons than he really was. And war is so many different things all jumbled together. It is hard to sort all these things out and give a sensible answer to one particular question.

To tell about my war I must go back in my memory many years. In the past few years I have dreamed about war, but I've rarely thought about it. Some names and places and events have gone, fuzzed over by dreams and wishes. But some knowledge has stayed with me. I know that, of the thousands and millions of men who fight a war, the true burden falls on only a few—the riflemen. Sometimes machine-gunners take it; and on rare occasions a

scout, runner, medic, stretcher-bearer or weapons special-
ist takes his share. But usually the rifleman takes it. I
know, too, that every man has his limit; but just as some
men are taller and heavier, so some men can go longer and
take more. There is a great spread among men. Some can
take very little; some take much. I don't know why. It does
not seem to depend on size or strength or intelligence, or
the lack of it.

Before a man goes into battle it is hard to say what he
will do. The last man to be able to say what he will do is
that man himself. Bravery is a fickle thing. It runs in some
kind of cycle: it comes and it goes. One day a man is a lion
in the fight; the next day a mouse. Stephen Crane showed
he knew that, in *The Red Badge of Courage*, even though
he had never been in war himself. *The Red Badge of
Courage* is the only book of war that ever meant anything
to me.

I haven't intended to write a book about bravery, even
though that is the quality, or lack of it, that most people
associate with war. I have seen men who were brave when
their feet were dry, cowards when they were wet; brave
when they were warm, cowards when they were cold;
brave when they were full, cowards when they were
hungry; brave as long as they got their sleep, but cowards
when they didn't. We often contrast bravery and cowardice. We think there is nothing between the two, but most
men who know war know that there is.

There is the way I dreamed I fought, and the way I
wish I had fought. There is also the way I think I fought,
and that is the story I have told here.

Essentials of the Organization
of the First Marine Division
During the Pacific Fighting in 1943-1944

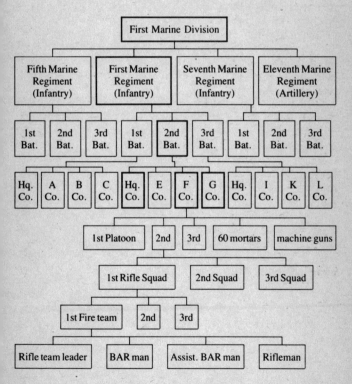

AUTHOR'S NOTE

The names and numbers of Marine units in this story require a word of explanation. The division here is the First Marine Division. The three infantry regiments in the First Division were: the First Marine Regiment (called "the First Marines"), the Fifth Marine Regiment (called "the Fifth Marines") and the Seventh Marine Regiment (called "the Seventh Marines"). In each regiment there were three infantry battalions: First Battalion, Second Battalion and Third Battalion. In each battalion there were a Headquarters Company and three rifle companies or "line companies" which were designated by letters: First Battalion (A, B and C Companies); Second Battalion (E, F and G Companies); Third Battalion (I, K and L Companies).

The author served in F Company, Headquarters Company and G Company of the Second Battalion, First Marines (Regiment), First Marine Division. "First Marines" always refers to the Regiment, and never to the Division.

SIBERIA
SEA OF
OKHOT
MANCHURIA
KURILE
KOREA
Seoul
Tokyo
JAPAN
RYUKYU IS.
Okinawa
BURMA
CHINA
Hong Kong
FORMOSA
Iwo Jima
THAILAND
LUZON
PHILIPPINE
ISLANDS
INDOCHINA
MARIANAS IS.
Saipan
Tinian
Guam
MARSHAL
Yap I.
Ulithi Is.
Palau Is.
Truk
CAROLINE ISLANDS
MALAYA
MINDANAO
Singapore
BORNEO
NEW GUINEA
SOLOMO
New Britain
JAVA
IS.
CORAL
SEA
Pavuvu
INDIAN OCEAN
New Caledonia
Noume
AUSTRALIA
Melbourne

1

AMPHIBIOUS ATTACK

September 15, 1944

The battleships tongued fire and slammed and the island rolled in smoke and orange light. As our transport went in, we hung at the rail and yelled at Peleliu: "Burn! Burn!"

So the war began for me. Dark chunks of Peleliu squirted up through the smoke. My face felt warm and itchy, and my hands were shaking, but I was not afraid. I didn't think about dying and I didn't think of the Japanese who were dying on the island, and those are the first two things wrong about war. I wanted to cheer, but I was too awed by the sound to do any more than what the others were doing. With them I chanted, "Burn!"

I watched the "old" men who had been through it before. Buck, the scout sergeant, stood up on a life raft and steadied himself with a hand on my shoulder while he leaned far out to watch. The F Company riflemen were chanting behind us. Buck said nothing. He looked. Then he said: "I've never seen a shelling like this."

We were like small children as we watched the Fourth of July display of our lives. Nobody was tense then, and nobody showed anything but wild excitement and great curiosity. We argued about which streamers were from the sixteen-inch guns, and we argued whether or not the battleship *Pennsylvania* was the big dragon that was tonguing out fire behind us. We jumped at the flash and slam from the gun muzzles, jumped again when the shell hit and shook the island, but we paid no attention to the damaging, dangerous birds that scurried overhead in the dark sky.

An hour before we had eaten breakfast, a stand-up meal of black coffee and dry toast, and one apple or one orange for each man. Some men grabbed more than one from the baskets at the stairway. We were crowded through the mess hall and out to the ladder and up to the deck of our transport, an LST (Landing Ship Tank). We slept on cots under an LCI (Landing Craft Infantry) that was lashed on blocks above the deck of the LST. We sat on our cots; Buck and John, the other scout sergeant, loaded magazines for their Tommy guns. I carried an M-1 rifle, and the clips came loaded.

I had said: "They told me they served steak and eggs before a landing."

Buck had laughed and said: "It's better not to have much in your stomach, in case you get hit."

The OP (Observation Post) runner jumped off his cot and scooted out on to the deck. That had been the first sign of tension in any of us, and when the OP runner ducked away from us, Buck and John had looked at each other without saying anything. We were loading magazines when the shelling began.

After the naval shelling began, our LST moved more slowly toward the transport area. The first excitement was over, and some of the men moved back from the rail and went to sit on their cots. It wasn't light enough to see faces, except out on the open deck when the gun flashes lighted everything. In the darkness under the LCI, cigarettes glowed and marked out the men who sat on their cots talking quietly or just thinking or praying.

When a lull came in the firing, and it seemed very quiet, Buck's voice

M1

sounded extra loud as he asked John: "You want to say some prayers?"

"No," John said. "I don't think so. At least, not out loud."

Buck didn't argue. The lull lasted long enough to hear the click of his Rosary beads as he turned them through his fingers. Then the firing began again, heavier than before. I had thought that men got more religious just before a battle, but it didn't seem to be that way. Buck was always religious, even in rest areas far from the lines; but John never was that I noticed.

The engines slowed and our LST rolled on its flat bottom in the swell that came off the island with dawn and the turn of the tide. I listened to pieces of conversation pounded down in the darkness by the sledge-beats of the guns:

"My brother had this Buick, see, and it cost him . . ."

"So my buddy says to her . . ."

"Our Father Who art in Heaven . . ."

"I was on my way into Tulsa at the time. . . ."

There was no mention of the war and no mention of the Marines or glory. Somebody told a joke. Somebody laughed, but softly. We went on into the transport area with shells shrieking overhead in the dawn sky.

Something screamed down on us and I rolled over on my cot and gripped the wooden bar at the end. I didn't yell. "Air strike," Buck said. He scrambled out toward the rail. "I want to see this."

Our air support had driven down over our transport line, and waves of planes were swinging toward the beach. It was a rocket and strafing run, and the noise of the diving planes was fearful. The ships opened up again. Some officer made a futile sputter over the deck speaker, but nobody could hear the words.

We lined up along the rail again. Some of the newer men had their packs on and their rifles slung. But most of the older men waited for orders from the deck speaker. The old men showed no fear on their faces or in their speech, but when I knew more about war I realized that some of them were screaming inside. And the tension settled among them. I could feel it when I brushed against John. Tension had made his body as unyielding as the steel plates of the deckhouse. In the light from the burning foreshore, I noticed that Buck seemed loose; but he was chewing steadily on his lip. Fear broke out in all kinds of ways in different men; some drooled like children, others seemed to itch; some men hid their heads in blankets or ponchos, and I knew a man who sucked his thumb when he was under fire. We watched a file of rocket-firing landing craft go by us toward shore. A destroyer, like a mother duck, led them.

Then, before we heard any word from the deck speaker, we heard the armored amphibious tractors start up down in the tank deck. They must have started them all at once, because the deck plates shook.

Buck said: "Well . . . We might as well get ready now. We must be nearly in."

There was no more talk among the old men. They drifted away from the rail toward their packs and weapons.

I helped John on with his pack. He was stiff and awkward with his arms. He said: "I can get it on all right."

"That's all right," I told him. "You're pretty old. I'm always glad to help an old man."

He didn't make any joke out of it. He mumbled: "I'm pretty old for this kind of thing."

I had trouble getting John's arms through the packstraps. He couldn't seem to bend them. I caught fear from the men around me. I was deeply shamed for them and for myself. Later I got used to fear. It was like a scar or a limp that I had to learn to live with. I learned always to control what showed in my face, my hands and my voice. And I let it rage on inside. I never lost my fear, but I lost my fear of fear, because it became such a familiar thing.

We were all lined along the rail, but we scarcely looked at the island. The show was stale, and nobody was interested any more. The noise racked nerves and set a tingle of fear that began like a toothache coming on slowly. The first platoon of F Company riflemen started into the hatchway to go down to the tank deck. I had heard no

Amtrac

order on the speaker, but perhaps it had come down the line from man to man.

Bob, one of our scouts who was going in with the platoon, called from the hatchway: "They're going to let me run the machine gun on the amtrac going in." Bob was an old machine-gunner and he was proud of it; he had a good reputation as a combat man.

"Keep the gun pointed toward shore," Buck warned him. "I remember when you got rattled on the Tenaru and turned your gun on G Company."

The scout said: "You think I'm a coward, you should meet my brother Denny. He's the family champion. But then he's older than I am and he's had more practice being yellow."

I had heard the scout and others say the same line many times before. It was a classic joke among the old men in the scout section. But this time nobody even smiled. I wanted to say something funny back to the scout, but by the time I got it out he had gone down into the hatchway. In combat outfits men almost never used the word "coward," except as a joke and usually about themselves. I never remember anyone being called a coward in anger. No one felt that sure of himself.

A rifleman from Massachusetts went by us. He said

out of the corner of his mouth to Buck: "You lucky rear-echelon guys! I wish I was a noncombatant like you." He said it half as a joke, but there was some serious feeling behind it. Men always turned on the men who were a foot or two behind them and a foot or two safer and teased them for being safe. We weren't offended. We would do the same to men who were safer than we were. We were Combat Intelligence scouts in a Marine Infantry battalion. It wasn't a safe job, but it was safer than the rifleman's. No job was worse than a rifleman's. So Buck, the old rifle squad leader, said nothing to the young rifleman.

I said to the rifleman: "Good luck, Joey."

He said: "Same. I wish this was Revere Beach or something."

The line shuffled forward and the light overhead was growing, and when it came it took the color and life out of men's faces. The noise became so steady that we forgot about it for a while. We just raised our voices higher and shouted above the racket. John had been yelling in my ear. I couldn't hear him and I turned to face him. He was asking me about the OP runner. I looked along the line and couldn't see him. Buck walked up ahead and couldn't find him. We went back under the LCI—and he was sitting on his cot staring at his pack and rifle.

"Get it on," Buck told him.

"I don't know whether I can."

"We'll help you," Buck said. He picked up the pack, spread out the straps with his hands.

"I mean I don't know whether I can go in."

"You don't have any choice. There's no other place in God's world for you to go but in." Buck began to stuff the runner's arms through the shoulder-straps.

As soon as the man had his pack on he flopped back on the cot. He was crumpled and limp, with his arms splayed out.

"Get up and get in line," Buck ordered him.

"I want to pray." That was the first time I had ever heard the runner mention praying.

Buck blew up again. I suppose he had been holding

his own tension down all along and I hadn't noticed it. He screamed in the runner's face and shook his arms and tried to drag him off the cot. John came in under the LCI and crowded Buck gently aside. Together John and I got our arms under the runner's arms and walked him back to the rail. We were called to the hatchway.

Buck's argument with the runner upset me, and it upset him. I was pressed against him in the line, and he was still shaking. We went down the iron ladder to the tank deck, and I saw Buck touch the runner's shoulder and say something to him. But when the runner turned in the companionway, under a bare ceiling bulb, his face was awful to look at. There seemed no blood or life under the skin, and he appeared as a dead man some time in the water. Buck saw the runner's face and turned away from it as though it bore an ugly wound.

We filed along a ramp; the amphibious tractors were down in the well, shaking the plates and turning the air blue with exhaust fumes. From that day to this, the heavy smell of exhaust brings back memory of the war. I can watch war movies and listen to fireworks or thunder, and they mean nothing to my memory; but the heavy smell of exhaust still makes my palms sweat. In the hold, the sway from ground swell was more noticeable. Some men were already seasick. Some men got seasick at the sight of small boats.

In each of the amtracs (amphibious tractors) there was a cardboard sign on a stick, and the signs had wave and boat numbers on them. We found our number, and Buck and I loaded. John and the runner went to another boat. John had lost his tenseness in his worry over the scared runner. There was a second runner, Larry, a moonfaced German boy from the Midwest, and he wasn't scared at all. Buck said to Larry: "See if you can get some moxie into your buddy there. He looks like he's ready to quit."

Larry grinned. "I'd quit too if I knew where we handed in our notice."

A squad of riflemen had already loaded into our amtrac. There was a spare radioman and two wiremen with phones and lines for the Observation Post. We got

LST

front places up near the squad leader, who was an old
friend of Buck's from Guadalcanal days. I put my hand on
a long metal ridge that ran down the middle of the tractor.
It was probably a propeller shaft housing. A rifleman next
to me said: "That thing will get hot after a while."

"So will everything else," Buck told him. We were in
a half-crouch, inside the metal case of the amtrac. When
the signal came, they would open the bow doors of the
LST, and we would ride all the way into the beach in the
armored tractor. We were in a reserve platoon and sched-
uled to come in with the third wave. That gave me no
comfort. Buck had explained that the third wave was
worse than the first, because the Japs had a chance to get
their heads up after the beach shelling stopped. "They
always shoot better at the third and fourth waves," Buck
explained. Buck always looked on the worst side of things.
Most men were optimists. They knew that some men
would get killed and crippled, but they were sure that it

would be somebody else and not they themselves. Only by thinking that way could they face combat. Buck was a pessimist. He thought that if he talked about the worst it wouldn't happen. He told me that in all of his four campaigns he always prepared himself to die, and expected it, but deep inside he hoped it wouldn't happen.

Buck pushed the muzzle of a BAR (Browning Automatic Rifle) away from his face. To the BAR man he said: "Will you keep that thing out of my eyes?"

"What's there to see?" the BAR man asked.

"Stand it up between your knees," Buck told the automatic rifleman. "I don't want to get my head blown off by some boot of a BAR man."

The squad leader snapped something at the BAR man and he shifted the position of his long rifle. There was some talking but then it all stopped. I was glad to have Buck in the same boat with me. In a war, loyalties shrink down past country and family to one or two men who will be with you. They become more important than anyone else in the world, more precious than father and mother, sister and brother, wife and girl. Only a few lonely mad men go through a war without buddies.

We heard the bow doors open. Chains scraped. The man beside me stiffened so suddenly that he caught my knee against the steel side of the tractor. I tapped him on the top of the helmet and he slowly relaxed and let out a long breath. No one seemed very relaxed except the radioman. He was fiddling with the dials on his set and pulling on the antenna. He had a job, something to do with his mind and hands, and I envied him. I opened my map case and studied the overlay of our landing beach area. We had sketched in gun positions from the aerial photographs. There seemed to be one black cluster of symbols for guns and bunkers all the way across our beach. The map didn't cheer me. I put it away.

The bow doors were open and the ramp was down, but we didn't move. Some fresh air eddied through the blue fumes of exhaust that lay in layers of different shades above us. Somebody said: "Let's go, before we die from monoxide."

"We'll go soon enough," someone assured him. I was wedged in so tight I couldn't turn to look at the man who spoke. I could only see the man who sat across the amphibious tractor from me. He looked miserable. He was hunched down into his jacket as far as he could go. His eyes streamed from the monoxide, and his teeth were clenched as though he were fighting an urge to scream or be sick.

A whistle sounded. The tracks began to rumble forward on the wooden carpets. We lurched forward, about the length of a track, and then stopped. The amtrac driver was talking to the Marine who manned the bow machine gun. I heard the machine-gunner's high squeaky voice, and I recognized it. He was a skinny blond boy, who looked about fifteen—and may have been. The men called him "Wingy." Wingy had been in the Intelligence scout section, but Buck had transferred him out to a rifle platoon. Wingy couldn't read a map; and he didn't care much anyway. Each day he wrote the same letter to twelve different girls back in the States. Buck didn't like Wingy because he never wrote to his mother, and all over the tent Wingy put up pictures that Buck tore down.

Wingy was standing up looking over his gun, and he was describing what he could see to the rest of us.

"They've started down the ramp. Some splash when they hit the water there! Hey, the Old Man is finally loading into his boat. He must have overslept. Let's go, hey!"

Buck said to the squad leader: "Why did you put that crazy kid on the gun? That nut, Wingy, there?"

"He volunteered," the squad leader said. "You want the job?"

"No," Buck said. "I just hope you locked the swivel so he can't turn the gun this way." To me, Buck said: "When we hit the beach, get over the side and run straight in. Don't stay near this thing. Don't hide behind it. It will be a fat target for those guns up on the high ground behind the airport."

"All right," I said. We started to roll forward again, and this time we seemed to be going out.

"We're going out," Wingy yelled. "Hang on! Hey, Buck, you look sick."

"You stupid boot," Buck snarled.

When we started down the ramp all the riflemen were spilled toward the front and we had to fight them off to breathe. I saw nothing for a moment but bright spots behind my eyelids, and heard nothing but a roaring in my head. I came close to fainting. Everyone on the boat was stiff with dread. But Wingy kept up his chatter even when we splashed into the water near the bow of the LST. The sky overhead was light, and signs of a big fire were in the air. Even far out, ash and smoke drifted overhead.

Wingy said: "Will you look at it, hey? The whole stinking island is burning."

"Never mind that," Buck said. "Do you see any splashes offshore? Are they firing back? Have any of our amtracs started in?"

"I can't see," Wingy said. "It looks like the first wave is going in. But it looks like those are empty."

I tried to lift my head above the gunwales of the amtrac. I needed air. "Stay down," Buck shouted. "Keep your head low."

My need for air was greater than any fear. Somebody was already sick in the boat, and I was almost ready to be. I pushed up until my eyes were level with the ledge below the gunwale. I peeped over. I could see nothing but smoke rolling off the island. It hung in a pall above the beach.

Fortifications and the concrete fangs of tetrahedrons showed above low water. Shellbursts blew gaping mouths in the smoke, and the dark and rotted teeth of the island ridge showed through. There were flashes against the ridge as the barrage lifted from the beach and rolled in on the high ground. The air overhead hummed with fire. Planes screamed and dived all along the transport line, and as they scaled in over the line of the beach they slipped and dipped and ran fast like ugly sea-birds. The ships of the line put out their tongues of fire toward the island. The sea was full of small craft and there was oil slick on the water. Ahead of us I saw the amtracs form into an irregular line between the picket boats. Then the line wheeled, and I saw white water from its wake as it turned in toward shore.

"There they bloody well go," Wingy howled. "Save some for us, hey?"

Buck was waving me down. "Get down low," he bellowed. I wedged myself down again but I couldn't stay there. My head jerked out of control as though somebody had it on a string. I popped up again. So did many of the others who could not ride into a beach blind, and without knowing what was ahead. Buck had no curiosity that was not necessary for his job.

The tension in the boat snapped as the men struggled up into fresh air. They peered over the side and yelled. The football game excitement came back. There was relief because it was too late to back out. We were out on the water, ready to go in on a defended beach—and there was no turning back, for even the biggest coward.

We went quietly into line, backing and plunging a bit in the surf like race horses in the starting gate. The control officers in the picket boats sighted along the line and then waved us ahead. We took off into the wake of the second wave, but it was hard to see them when they were in the troughs of the swells. Everyone was up and yelling but Buck and the squad leader. They crouched low; both of them were young but their faces looked old with determination and fear. When we hit the beach they would have the job to do, and we would do whatever they told us to do.

It was almost a glorious feeling, roaring in toward the beach with fear gone for the moment. We were in motion with thousands of tons of armed might at our backs; and it seemed that nothing could stop us. We were an old and tried outfit, led by men like Buck and the squad leader, who would know what to do when the time came to do it. As we rolled in on Peleliu, and before we were hit, the excitement took us and we were not afraid of anything. Some men began to chant: "Drive! Drive! Drive!"

I saw the amphibious tractor in front of us go up in a shellburst. For a moment I didn't realize what I had seen. Somebody said: "Hey, I think they hit him," in a complaining tone, as though it were against the rules to do that.

The amtrac flamed, spread gas on the water, and wallowed in a puddle of fire. Men spilled from it. The driver of our tractor screamed so loud we heard him above everything. He had seen the hit and he was very frightened. Wingy also screamed, begging for an order to open fire with the machine gun.

The squad leader bellowed at him: "You crazy kid, there's nothing in front of you but our own guys. If you fire one burst I'll chop you down."

The first shell came in and hit in our wake. It sprayed water all over the men in the rear and slewed the back of the amtrac around. The driver fought it straight and we went on. But now we were all trying to cram ourselves back down inside the steel sides. And there was less space, for some reason. Quiet fear shrinks men; wild fear expands them.

Small-arms fire racketed along our side. A man's shoulder showed a puff and then a dark stain, and he clasped it with his other hand and swore briefly.

Buck said: "Machine guns. How can they reach us out here?"

Buck and the squad leader had jumped up when the return fire began. They were the best kind of old men, who never left an inch of themselves exposed when there was nothing to be done. But when there was trouble they were up.

The squad leader stumbled over heads and fell toward Wingy. "What's going on, kid? Are they reaching us?"

Wingy turned his thin face, and it was all big eyes. The rest of his features had retreated. "They're hitting them all," he said. Again he complained, as though it were against the rules. "What will we do?"

"Fire at that near point," the squad leader ordered.

"Keep high." Wingy fumbled with the belt and slide, trying to full-load. But he didn't fire. He stood up straight and then fell over among the men. And he seemed to vanish. I don't remember seeing Wingy again, but he must have still been in the amtrac. People and things dropped suddenly out of sight in action. Or at least the memory of them did. The squad leader and Buck began to feed and fire the machine gun.

Fire chopped and roiled the sea around us, and water sloshed in over the gunwales and steamed on the hot metal. Some men were crouched down but others pressed their faces in against the steel sides. We were bumping on something underneath. Buck and the squad leader fired on. The radioman started a gobbling call into his set, even though he couldn't have been getting through to anyone. The tracks bumped on, hitting high places in the sand underneath the water. The tracks would hit, grind, spin, and then kick into free water throwing high geysers as the whole amtrac shot forward.

"I can't get any farther in," the driver yelled. "Get out of here, before we get hung up."

"Get in," Buck yelled. "Get on in farther, or I'll blow you into the water."

The driver yelled and pleaded. He said he had to unload and go back for more. He wasn't doing anybody any good, he said, if he got hung up on the sand. We were all drenched. Another round came in and scattered shrapnel across the back of the boat, but somehow nobody was hit. Many things may have happened, but I caught only a few flashes. I saw a shell land right in the amtrac beside us. It tipped on its nose and men spilled into the water. Then were were on sand and the tracks were spitting under water. "Unload," the driver begged us. "I can't go any more. I'll never get off."

"Drop your ramp," the squad leader told him. He and Buck were firing the machine gun but looking behind them at the men. Smoke rolled down on us, and I had no idea how far we were from the shore. The ramp went down, but the driver panicked and tried to back out before anybody could unload. He seemed terrified that he would

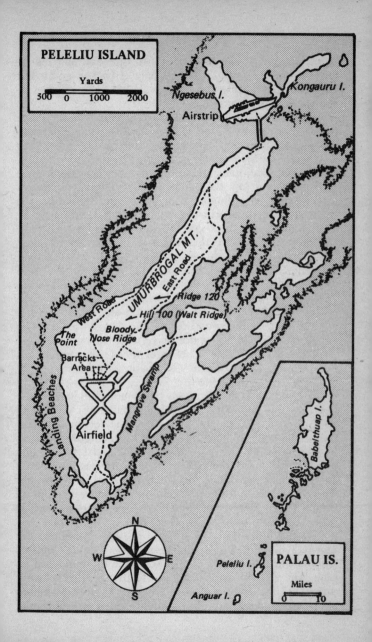

hang the tractor and himself up on the sand and not be able to get out again. He fiddled and backed and a few riflemen jumped into the water; one was scythed down by the swing of the ramp.

The squad leader left the gun and ran along the ledge below the gunwale. "Out!" he yelled at the men. "Get out! They've zeroed-in on every amtrac in this line."

Some men were willing to go, but they didn't know which way. One man jumped right over the side, but he lost his rifle. I saw the squad leader stepping on fingers and kicking at helmets. Somewhere in the mess, the radioman yelled: "Careful of my equipment, you fools."

"Drive 'em," Buck said. "Before we get hit good." We started to push toward the back and the riflemen fell away toward the ramp. Only one man hesitated at the edge of the ramp. He screamed that he could not swim. We were pushing him—and then the shell hit. It must have hit between us, on the ramp, and it must have been a small mortar round. I didn't see it, or even afterwards remember the flash or the sound of it.

I came up in the water and I still had my rifle, my pack and my map case. The water must have been about waist-deep. I tore free of my gas mask. I couldn't see Buck or anybody else near me.

I caught a flash of amtracs burning in one long line. I had only one thought, to find Buck and find out what to do. . . . But I couldn't find him. I couldn't see anyone near me in the water. There must have been hundreds there; but my mind played some strange trick and I saw no one and thought I was alone. All I wanted to see was Buck.

I did not see Buck, but the memory of his voice was with me. I had heard him say a hundred times: "Run in on them. Don't stay at the water edge. Get ground under you." I began to slog in. Underwater, the beach was potted and full of holes. I stepped in deep places and fell more than once. But I don't remember seeing anyone. Around and above and everywhere the air hummed and sang. The zip, zip, zip became so steady it settled into one drone at high pitch. I ran into the humming smoke, floundering sometimes, but running on. Everything had shut down around me and I noticed nothing more but the loom of the land in the smoke, and the hum all around me.

I fell out of the water and on to the beach. Then I got up and flopped another five yards forward. The sand was gray and rough and littered with splintered palm trees and chunks of coral. For the first time I saw men around me. Later I learned that some of my closest and best friends died in the water off Beach White 2 in Peleliu. But I never saw them. I ran around them or stepped over them, and there was one great anxiety—where was Buck? I had run through some of the fiercest fire put down on any landing beach in the war, and flopped down on the shore, I lay catching my breath and worrying about Buck. I was on the beach, but I had no idea what to do next.

2

BEACHHEAD

Things changed on the beach. In the mist and smoke objects began to appear in detail. From the one high, whispering drone of passing death, individual sounds broke clear. Shell fire slammed in. Mortars *carrumped*. Small-arms fire picked its way through the heavier sounds. Men cried and called.

Great fear had emptied the world of faces for me, but suddenly they all came back into view. I was among men and things, on the beach. It was a very crowded beach. The gray sand was covered with litter: splinters of coconut log; fragments of coral, gas masks, helmets, broken weapons and mortar-shell cases—and of man himself, who was no more than litter on that beach.

An officer who described the place later reported a bloody, vicious scene, but I remember it differently. I remember the litter rather than any great horror. Many men had been hit there, but they weren't very noticeable. They quietly bled and died in the sand, without being conspicuous.

The first faces I noticed were strange ones. The men had daubed their cheeks with burnt cork and some kind of paint, and I knew they weren't from my battalion.

"What outfit you from?" I asked one of them.

"K Company," he said "K Company... Third Battalion, First."

I had come ashore in the wrong battalion area. My place was almost a company-front off, to the right. I began to move sideways and to my right, scooting a pace or two like a land crab and then falling into an empty hole. I was anxious to get away from the painted faces. The paint made them look like the most scared bunch of men I ever say. They scared me, just looking at them.

I was working into my own battalion area. The faces on the boundary were mixed, some painted and some plain. I almost fell over a man who was sitting on the sand watching the blood throb out of a mangled leg. He had started to tie a tourniquet around his leg, but the shock, or the strange fascination of watching his own blood pump out, intrigued him so much that he was simply staring down at the wound, without making any attempt to staunch the bleeding. I paused for a minute, benumbed by the sight of a man's lifeblood pumping out in regular, wavy rhythm. Then I got behind the man, reached around his waist and took his belt. I cinched his belt into his leg, just above the knee. He said nothing, and as though there were nothing more interesting to watch, after the bleeding had stopped, he rolled over on his side and lay there with his eyes open and staring. I stayed with him, yelling, until I could get a medical corpsman.

The corpsman said: "We ought to be getting an evac boat in here soon—I hope. This guy might just last and make it; then again he might not."

I waved at the corpsman to shush him, pointing down at the open eyes.

"He can't hear a thing we say," the corpsman said. "He's miles away in shock land."

"I'm going to move down to my outfit," I told the corpsman. He nodded and spat tobacco juice on the wounded man's shoes. That was tender nursing care in the Marines.

Moving through the litter of the beach, I was like a ragpicker in a dump. I exchange my M-1 for a Tommy gun and then swapped the Tommy gun for a BAR, and finally swapped back to an M-1 again. I had no purpose in swapping weapons; they were just lying around. I still had only one clear thought—to find Buck. I was certain that he would give me something to do and end my pointless

BAR

stumbling along that smoky beach. At that time Buck was my mother and father, sister and brother; and I needed him.

The first familiar face I saw was that of the scared OP runner. He was down on his hands and knees being sick into the sand. Beyond him was a man that for some reason I thought was Buck. I threw myself down beside the other man, seized his shoulder and turned his face toward mine; and I was looking directly into a great gaping hole where his face had been. It must have been the sight of that horror that had made the runner sick. I couldn't tell who the man was. There was no way to tell from what was left.

"Where's Buck"? I asked the runner. "Buck? Where is he? Or John? You came in with John. What happened to him?"

But the runner was too far gone in shock to answer. He shook his head and tears spun off to the side, and he said nothing. Perhaps he had known the faceless one.

I worked around the runner, although he clung to my knees as I tried to get by. The going was easier, but there was still a jumble of many companies. I kept asking for Buck. Some men didn't know. Some didn't even answer. I saw a redheaded corporal, flailing his heavy arms and urging the men forward into the smoke at the edge of the beach. The corporal seemed to know what he was doing and I pressed toward him, happy to attach myself to anyone who knew what he was supposed to do. He had a powerful voice backed up with sweeps of his thick, hairy arms.

"Get forward," he bellowed. "There's a ditch ahead. Get into it. Stop bunching up on that sand like sheep." He aimed a kick at one crawling rifleman. Other men began to shuffle forward, heavily loaded with equipment. But some men kept their heads buried in the sand. I saw the biggest, strongest man in the battalion, and fear had flattened him to the beach, where he lay without a weapon and with terrified eyes. I stepped over him and found a long deep trench that he couldn't get strength enough to reach.

The trench had been dug by the Japanese as an antitank defense and it was the best cover on the beach. In it the officers were forming up the platoons for an assault into the smoky jungle ahead. Battalion officers were all scrambled-in with riflemen and machine-gunners. The redheaded corporal came back through the smoke to the forward edge of the trench and called to some officer. 'We're pinned down—flat down. Is there a demolitionist here?"

A big, dark dynamiter popped up and yelled: "Hey, Red, I'm with you. I thought you'd never ask."

The dynamiter wore a pack with a skull and cross-bones and the word *DANGER* stenciled on it. When he left the trench, one of the riflemen beside me said: "I'm glad to see him go. When he gets hit he's going to go up with a real big bang."

Somebody in the trench kept repeating: "It's coming from the bunker on the point. We've got to take out that bunker on the point."

I recognized the voice. It was John's. He was perched up on top of the forward rim of the trench, peering off into the smoke and speaking over his shoulder to the major who was battalion executive officer. Both of them looked curious, rather than afraid, and I stumbled along the trench toward them.

"Where's Buck?" I asked John. "I think he got hit out in the water. I couldn't find him."

John said. "You're the one that's hit. Your face is covered with blood."

I didn't believe him. "Where's Buck?" I insisted. I put my hand up to my face and found it sticky with blood. I almost screamed aloud.

John took me by the shoulder and pressed me down against the bank. He said: "Buck's all right. He's just down the gully there. He thought you got hit out in the water. He was right at that." John had broken open a battle dressing and he was swabbing away at my forehead and face.

The major turned back from the smoke: "He hurt bad?" he asked John.

"I don't think so," John said. "Hold still, Dave, while I clear away the gore . . . Now. . . He's not hurt bad. Just a fat cut and a crease."

"Lucky guy," the major said.

As I sat against the bank, I began to realize that I had been hit, but I had no recollection of when it had happened. Either I had got creased when the shell landed out on the amtrac; or later on the beach one of the scurrying, buzzing things had taken off my helmet and furrowed along the side of my head. There was a long scratch there and blood caked all the way down inside my collar.

John poured water from his canteen and sponged away with the dressing. He was an artist in civilian life and he had deft fingers, even in battle. He cleaned the wound without giving me a twinge of pain.

"You'll do fine," he assured me. "Just one nick and no

hole." He shook sulfa powder on the wound and taped a pad over it. The side of my head felt numb but there was no pain. "I could pull it with tape," he said, "but I think you'll need a couple of stitches to hold it. Wherever you get your luck from, ask for a little for me."

As soon as he took his hand from my shoulder I stood up and looked around. "I don't see Buck," I told him. I thought John had been spoofing me to keep me quiet.

"You sure you're all right?" the major asked.

I mumbled something and stumbled away. I saw Buck. He and another man were bent over, working on the firing mechanism of a bazooka. Buck saw me and grinned over his shoulder. "The wires are wet or something. We'll need another."

The shells began to land on the back of the trench and scatter shrapnel all through it, and we dived for the bottom and lay there in a heap. Buck turned and yelled in my face: "I thought they got you, out in the water."

John was gritting his teeth as the shells landed, but he said: "This guy has real luck. I hope it holds." He rolled over on his back and fished out his canteen. "Drink some water," he ordered me. "I think they're lifting again."

It was like that in the trench. There would be a few minutes of furious fire down and then a few minutes of almost complete lull, although the small arms and the mortars never really stopped. I had a drink of water and sat up with a sick and dizzy head. I carried aspirin in my pack and I got out the little can and ate three of them and passed the can to Buck and John. They each had two.

Buck said: "We got to know where our flanks are. The whole line is scrambled." He looked at me. "Can you go out and find the right end of the line?"

I nodded. I was glad to get something to do. "Find out where and how it ties into the Fifth," John instructed me. I crawled away from them along the trench and worked onto the open beach, and once again I was in a buzzing world that was like a dream.

I worked across G Company and into E, where I stopped in a hole to watch two demolitionists at work. One of them, a white-haired old man called "Pop," was patiently fixing the fuze on a shape charge (demolition) while the air overhead buzzed. While he worked Pop was lecturing the young man with him, just as though they were in a schoolroom. I asked Pop where the line ended.

"I'm not sure," he said. "But we must be about at the end out here. Except for the boys working on that bunker on the point, the rest of them have swung inland." Pop patted his charge and said: "This will do it, lad. Don't crawl in without some covering fire. This baby will shake 'em real good."

I wriggled away toward the bunker. The assault men had it in its last stages. Riflemen worked all around it and some of them were in close to the wall, stuffing hand grenades through the fire ports. A flame-thrower man was trying to get the muzzle of his hose unplugged with a knife, and Pop's assistant was wriggling forward with his shape charge. Beyond a coral bunker, which had supported the main pillbox, a rifleman lay, burned black. He had been on the wrong side of the bunker when the flame-thrower went, and I could not tell if he was a Marine or a Jap. Somebody yelled: "Fire in the hole!" The flame-thrower man and I huddled together and there was a smashing sound and a tower of debris squirted up over our heads. I got up and began to run inland and collided with a rifleman diving in the same direction.

We ran over a low ridge of coral and through a fringe of palms and down into a swamp. The palms were still standing inland, and the Japanese fire was landing high up in the tops and scattering fronds and shrapnel down in the grove below. There was a cluster of riflemen, held up at a low ridge and facing a thicket. A squad leader pointed his finger at the thicket. Two riflemen worked around on either side of it while a BAR man chopped into the middle of the brush. There was a scurrying sound and the BAR man yelled: "Here they come!" I swung my Tommy gun and fired on the thicket and all the riflemen were firing into it, the leaves being chipped and lashed by the bullets. We all lay still. "We got 'em," the squad leader said. "Let's move out." I went forward with the riflemen because I didn't want to be left alone. I don't know what, if anything,

Flame Thrower

I hit in the thicket. I never looked or wanted to. A rifleman told me as we ran through a break in a low ridge and splashed through a puddle in a second swamp: "Lots of Japs in there. The Fifth Marines chased 'em into us. We got 'em."

On the other side of the swamp pool was a high bank that formed the edge of the airfield. Riflemen were going up over the bank as a platoon leader waved them on. The platoon leader saw me and called: "Where's the colonel?"

"In the big ditch on the beach."

"Get back and tell him we've hit the airfield and we can see the Fifth Marines moving up."

I walked back under the overhang of the bank. I

didn't want to run through the swamp alone, but the lieutenant was watching me and I had to go. Just beyond the puddle, one of our platoons, moving up, opened fire over my head. I yelled at them and told them that men were already ahead on the bank near the airfield. "Good-o," their lieutenant said. "This will go easier now we're off the beach."

Behind the reserve company John and the colonel were moving up with the battalion OP group. They were running and ducking into holes. I told them it was all clear to the airport. One of the OP wiremen said: "Well, that's good news."

He stood up straight and walked ahead two paces with his spool of wire. Then he sat down and looked silly. He had been hit in the shoulder by a sniper firing from the swamp. The rest of the OP team ran on to the bank and began to set up on the edge of the airport. John sent me to find Buck and get the position of the left side of our line.

Shells were still hitting high up in the palm trees when I went through. I decided not to crawl. I put my head down and ran through, expecting to get my helmet torn off by the shrapnel which was scaling down from overhead.

I didn't find Buck, but I found our lieutenant. I hadn't seen him since before the campaign. He had come up on a different ship. When I saw him I cut across to where he sat, half in a hole and with his back braced against a coconut tree. Before I got close to him I knew he had been shot. He had the slumped shoulders of a wounded man, and from close up his face looked pinched-in and white. Still he was unmarked, and no bandages or dressings showed. He recognized me and tried to smile. I saw then why he was bent over. Along his belt line ran a dark crease of blood. I knelt down beside him.

"Let me take a look," I told him.

He shook his head. "The corpsman has seen it. He's gone back to get help to get me out of here. It isn't bad."

"Are you sure?" I asked.

"I'm not sure, because I don't know and I didn't want

to look . . . But it doesn't feel bad." Shrapnel spilled down
out of the trees behind us and we both huddled in close to
the bole of the coconut.

"I could move you to a better place," I offered. "There's
a lot of stuff hitting up high in those trees."

He didn't say anything to that. He muttered: "I felt it
and there was something sticking out like pulp." He
shuddered.

"It's probably all right," I assured him. "Sure you
don't want me to look?" I didn't want to look or even to
touch his wound, but I had to make the offer. He didn't
answer me.

His eyes had begun to lose their focus. I sat with him
awhile. I offered him a cigarette which he refused, muttering
something about a pipe. I offered to fill his pipe but he
thought it would make him sick if he smoked. Sometimes
he made sense and sometimes he didn't. I figured that the
corpsman had put a shot of morphine into him, though I
wasn't sure and it didn't seem right to ask. He asked me
how things were going and I tried to tell him, but he kept
losing the trend and asking me to repeat details over and
over. He said quite clearly: "I'm cold." I covered his legs
and stomach with his poncho.

When the stretcher-bearers came for him I was holding him up with my shoulder so he wouldn't sprawl down
in the hole and break himself up any more. As they rolled
him on the stretcher, his eyes opened, and again he
recognized me. "You better go on, now," he said. He tried
to say something else, but at last he only waved his hand
slightly.

The lieutenant hadn't looked bad, but they never did
get him out. He died somewhere on the way to the
hospital ship, or on it. Later I wished that I had talked
more with him or said something comforting or helped
with his wound, but neither he nor I realized that he was
going to die. When I wrote a letter to his folks later I tried
to remember what we had talked about then or before,
but there never had been much. I never got to know him
or understand him very well, and at the last of it he never
said anything very gallant; and I hadn't said anything very

Sherman Tank

comforting. War is one of the few businesses where people talk shop while they are dying.

I met Buck and told him about the lieutenant. "Sounds like a gut wound," Buck said. "I hope he gets out of it all right. He never did anybody any harm."

Buck told me that one of our company scouts had been hit very hard going across the beach. We worked our way back through the palm trees and across the swamp to the edge of the airport. A lot of men were digging in behind the high bank. Heavy fire droned overhead from pillboxes across the field, but not much of it was landing near the bank. Machine-gunners and riflemen were moving out over the bank to dig in just on the edge of the airfield itself. We lay at the top of the bank, observing the blockhouse area across the field. We could pick out gun flashes in the smoke.

"We need tanks for those," Buck told me. "A couple

of Shermans could come right up here and knock holes in those walls."

The colonel crawled up beside us to look. He agreed with Buck. "Go back to the beach and bring up any tanks that have landed," he ordered me.

"I'll go," John offered. "You catch your breath."

"I'd better. There's only one break in the ridge and I know where it is." I rolled down the bank and started through the swamp. It looked as if I were going to be wearing a path through that swamp.

I was glad that a squad of riflemen were clearing out the snipers when I went through. They told me that they had one treed, "like a coon," but I didn't stop to watch them flush him out.

Things were no better on the beach. The heavy fire that poured over the bank was landing in the beach, which was still heaped with men and supplies and abandoned equipment. Somebody had laid about half a dozen dead near the water's edge, and there were wounded on stretchers, waiting for evacuation. Out on the shoals a line of amtracs still burned. As I walked upright, sand spewed up from mortar blasts or chipped away in flecks from rifle and machine-gun fire. A wounded man crawled on his knees and howled about something. I felt sorry for the wounded but I didn't look at them any more than I had to. Nothing I could do would have helped them. They had to wait and hope that they got out before something else landed on them. That was the worst part of a beach.

They were unloading tanks in the middle of the beach. They had swung them in on boats or barges, and there was confusion all around. Everybody offered different advice. I sat down on the sand to watch, and when fire poured down I lay down in the sand. I located a lieutenant of tanks and crawled over to him.

"I'd get 'em off the beach," I told him. "In fact, the colonel wants them up near the airport."

"Don't be crazy," he told me. "They never should have put them ashore."

"It's safer up there," I said. "At least there's cover. I know the way in."

The lieutenant looked at the tanks and the geysers of water and spurting sand from the shellfire. He had nothing to lose. Any place was better than that beach.

"You know a way?" he asked me.

I nodded. One tank unloaded and toiled up the incline of the beach. I ran across the sand and got up to the open turret. I had to yell in the tank commander's ear, but I couldn't convince him. The lieutenant got up on the tank with us and I began to talk to him.

"Look," I told him, "I'll ride up here all the way. I'll show you where to go."

That convinced the lieutenant. If I was willing to risk riding outside, he was willing to take a chance and order the tanks in.

I rode the tank along the beach, into the palms, through the break in the first ridge and down a stone path that was like a causeway through the first swamp. Only one sniper fired and he was on the wrong side of the turret, and I managed to duck down and hang on while the tankman buttoned up.

When we went through the grove the shells were still scaling down branches and shrapnel, and the driver had to duck down under the hatch. I jumped off the tank and ran ahead. Another tank was rumbling in behind us, and I waved the two of them up, and took them all the way to the bank.

When they got behind the bank the first commander opened up the hatch and got out. "What a ride!" he said. "How'd you like it out there?"

"I didn't. But I got you here. Come on up the bank and I'll show you some targets."

When the tank man and I came up the bank I got the first commendation I received in the war. Not from the colonel, who had other things on his mind, but from Buck and John, whose praise meant more. "Good work," John said. "I never thought you'd get them up here."

"He's a good man," Buck said. "What did I tell you? He's hard nose." Buck and John began to call targets to the tank men, and I went down to the foot of the bank to rest.

In the early afternoon we opened our rations and ate our first meal on Peleliu. It was hard cheese, dust-dry crackers, and lemonade which we mixed in our canteens from little packets of powder. The Marines called it "battery acid," and it tasted like it. As we ate, it seemed as though the misery of the beach was all behind us. Under the bank it was quiet. Shells passed over from us to them and from them to us; but most of it went from the hills to the beach, and only a few rounds landed in the mushy swamp behind the bank.

After I ate, I began to relax. In fact I relaxed too much and became almost silly. I called at people I knew and tried to kid Buck, who was getting glum. But Buck was hard to cheer up. He kept talking of the friends he had lost on the beach. We all had lost friends on the beach, and perhaps it was a heartless thing to be happy in those circumstances, but most of the men were. The young riflemen were laughing and calling names at the machine-gunners who were tugging up wire for their fortifications. When a small lull comes on the line it almost seems as if the war is over.

I noticed that Buck and John and some of the older men weren't laughing or joking at all. The old sergeants were hurrying around with belts of machine-gun ammunition draped in shiny necklaces over their shoulders. They were driving men up over the bank with jerry cans of water, boxes of rifle ammunition and grenades. Back near the light mortars, carrying parties were coming in with more ammunition. A sergeant of machine guns was bellowing: "Dig it in. Dig it down. Get that wire out." A rifle sergeant was hollering: "Come on, boy, you just scratched that ground. Get that BAR dug in." A lieutenant went along the line straightening it, waving men forward and back to places with better cover. All of this finally got through my silly mood and I realized that something was coming.

"What's up?" I asked Buck. "Why all the fuss? This is

the quietest it's been since the landing." I was leaning back on the bank, sunning myself.

Buck looked at John. "It's quiet," Buck agreed. "Too bloody quiet."

"Quiet is the way I like it," I said.

"Not this kind of quiet," John said. "I had a look into the pillbox area and something is forming up out there."

I watched a machine-gunner dragging a concertina of barbed wire up the bank. He was cursing the needle-sharp barbs that stuck in his hand. The signs were up: the line was bracing for a heavy attack.

"We may see a Banzai charge," Buck said.

"Maybe not a Banzai," John said. "Even the Japs have learned that those don't work. But we will see a counter-attack, maybe even with tanks. *Something* is throwing up the dust out there."

"When will it come?" I asked. My happy mood was gone. I noticed that even the young riflemen had stopped their noise and there was quiet all along the line—except for the sergeants, who were saying: "Dig. Dig."

"Hard to say when it will come," John said. "But I think soon. We'd best defend along this bank. Get yourself a slot."

Buck hitched up the bank beside me. "When it comes, don't move. Don't raise up and don't run. Face ahead and try to hit something." He tipped his head up toward the sky and listened to the drone of the incoming shells. "It's getting heavier," he said.

I could hear carrumping down in the swamp as though some heavy-footed giant were pacing toward us. "They're walking mortars back through the swamp toward us," Buck said. "Just stay loose. I don't think they'll get much shrapnel effect on that soft ground. The stuff will just sink in." He touched my shoulder and hitched back to his own slot. He began to arrange BAR magazines along the bank. I noticed that he had got an automatic rifle from somewhere. It was the best kind of weapon to have in that place. I moved down the bank and exchanged my short-range Tommy gun for an M-1 and three slings of ammunition.

I faced ahead, trying to see across the airstrip into the

pillbox area. There the shelling stirred up black cyclones of dust, and through that dust would come the attack—men and tanks. Already our tanks were throwing plunging fire directly across, trying to break up the attack before it formed. I had a strong urge to run, but by then there was no direction to run in. The mortars walked behind us. I spread out my arms and hugged the bank as though I were afraid I would fall off. Behind the dust and the smoke the attack built, sending its dusty signs towering into the sky, and rolling a menacing cloud ahead of it.

3

TAKING THE ATTACK

An attack sneaks up, covered by its own noise. The artillery rolls down in waves, but it takes a while to realize that the waves are not cresting or breaking and rolling away. The waves just keep thundering in. Mortars walk clumsily, thumping and carrumping, but suddenly they begin to stumble in everywhere, into deep holes and behind high walls. Mortars are deadly, like a clumsy man handling explosives, because they can bumble in anywhere, and when they get in close there is no more of the clumsy sound—only a deadly swish and an explosion that nobody close-in ever hears. Rifle fire picks its way daintily, but when it builds up it comes stinging in from all sides, and you get the illusion that it is circling and swirling like hiving bees. Machine guns pour a high-pressure jet of sound. It all builds up together until suddenly you realize that the attack is on you, and that each whispering bullet is aimed at *you*.

Buck said: "It's here. Don't run and don't move."

I plastered myself to the top of the bank beside a scrub palm that had been felled by shellfire. When I raised my head, small-arms fire came winging and stinging in and pulled splinters from the tree trunk beside me. Then, only after thousands of rounds of fire had been poured around me, I realized what bullets did. They ripped and tore, and flesh is weaker than palm log. I put my fingers up to the scratch along the side of my forehead, remembering what had almost happened before. The scratch was still sore. I buried my head between the bank and the log.

Someone panicked and I heard him scrambling down from the bank. Buck yelled: "Lie in there, you gutless wonder." The scrambling stopped. I did not turn my head to see who he yelled at. Whoever it was felt the same as I did. Our line opened up and the noise was much worse than the income fire. I was scared but I could not keep myself from raising up to peer into the smoke that was rolling across the airport. Some of the F Company riflemen were falling back in front of the attack, but still there were no clear signs of the Japs. They were out there somewhere, moving in behind the smoke. But they were coming. The forward riflemen were running back, like animals galloping before an oncoming forest fire. Two machine-gunners came walking in, carrying their gun still mounted. They never once looked back into the smoke and they appeared thoughtful rather than scared. There was remarkably little confusion, and no panic. The First Marines were a highly skilled defensive regiment, and had been since the Battle of the Tenaru on Guadalcanal. "We'll bust them," Buck yelled from beside me. "We'll bust them wide open."

An officer stood up and waved his hands. "What's he doing?" John yelled.

Buck bellowed: "Maybe he's lost or something." Buck began to fire, squeezing his bursts off in patterns of fours and fives, the way a good BAR man should. He reached for another magazine from the supply he had stacked along the bank. John kept his Tommy gun and he was not firing because he could hit nothing at long range. He listened to Buck fire and said: "You can still play that instrument, Bucko."

"Hear those bursts," Buck said. "My mother didn't waste that dough she put out for my violin lessons." Off to the right a new man poured out a long, barrel-burning burst on his BAR. "Miserable boot," Buck said, "He'll be shooting around corners with that thing by the time he sees a Jap." He turned toward me: "Pick and fire, boy. This is the only time you really earn your room and board."

I suddenly realized that I had a rifle in my hands. I aimed into the smoke and began to pick away at any dark looming shape that looked likely. The first targets were low and dark and they seemed to bounce high in the smoke. I had no idea what they were but I tracked and fired.

"Tanks," John called. "Small ones, but there will be foot-men running in behind them."

I fired on, and all thought of incoming fire had gone from my mind. There were pitching, bucking, wheeling shapes in the smoke and I wanted to hit them, and when one of them flamed up in the gray and rolled on its nose I had a feeling of keen pleasure, and I was sure I had stopped it with my own fire. Later I realized that was unlikely; but then I believed it, and hundreds of other riflemen believed the same thing.

Two bazooka men posed on the lip of the bank like circus performers getting ready for a high-wire balancing act. The rear man loaded and wired the piece, and the front man aimed and triggered, and a slow shot went out toward the first tank, already clearly discernible directly in front of us. There was flame along the front of the tread and the tank stopped and toppled over. One of the bazooka men cheered like a little boy: "Yay! Yay! That's us!"

Two Japanese wriggled out of the tank and started their dash through the swirling smoke. One was plastered against the tank before he could take three steps. The other got clear and began to dash laterally along the line. He must have been hit with a hundred rounds as he went into a somersault, a roll from the momentum, and a very dead sprawl.

Then the action came in on top of us and the rest was a blur. I saw a demolitionist run forward with a satchel charge, but he disappeared and I never saw him plant it. A machine-gun squad came tumbling in beside me and they began to fire without bracing the legs of the gun. The gun kicked itself all over the top of the bank while two of

Japanese Model 95 Light Tank

the squad tried to pin it down and the gunner cursed them and fired on.

A dark, clanking thing shot over the top of the bank a few yards away and cut a swath through the line, rolling men and weapons before it. I turned and was amazed to see a Jap tank that had come right over the bank. Men whirled around and poured fire into the tank, which had gone nose-down in the swamp. Its oil slick spread out on the swamp pool, but I did not see it begin to burn, and no one got out of it that I saw.

A man came running back, then stumbling back, then crawling back to collapse directly in front of my rifle. Buck and I crawled out to get him, and Buck rolled him over and put his head on the man's chest. Buck shook his head at me. We crawled back and left the dead man there. All around there was firing and running and rearing and the swirl of exhaust and the smell of powder, and a steady hammer-beat from the 75's on our tanks. The beat of the

75's was the worst of all noises because the tankers plunge-fired right over us in a point-blank slugging match with the Japanese. During all the fight the smoke never lifted very high. It constantly changed in thickness as our smoke and theirs blended and shifted with whatever breeze or blast there was.

The attack lifted in the same way it had come on. The artillery waves crested and broke and left a calm backwash still ringing with after-echo. The mortars stumbled back into the smoke, and the steady drone of small arms swirled away. And it was quiet.

Men turned away from their firing positions and wiped the sweat from their eyes with a handkerchief or the sleeve of their dungarees. A few began to chatter to fill the sudden silence. I turned away from my rifle and stretched full length on the bank. I was trembling all over. I tried to light a cigarette but I had trouble managing the pack. I fumbled two of them on the ground, ripped my dry lip with the third, and burned my chin with the wavering match. But I had one going finally and I lay back and drove smoke up at the dirty sky overhead. The attack had probably lasted five minutes. Of that total I remembered no more than two minutes of it. I felt as though I had been lying in one place for hours and my shoulder ached and my eyes watered and smarted.

All along the line men stood up again. I started to.

"Keep down," John warned me. His voice seemed terribly loud and had a ring to it. "They're still firing. It just *seems* quieter."

Along the line came the hoarse and hateful cry: "Corpsman! Corpsman!" That cry frightened me then, and the memory of it still frightens me. It is the worst Greek chorus sound of war.

John pulled the magazine of his Tommy gun. He flicked two shells off the top with his thumbnail and tossed the empty magazine over his shoulder. Buck was sorting through the BAR magazines beside him. I hadn't remembered firing much, but there were half a dozen ejected clips beside me on the bank. A rifleman bent over the dead man in front of us, checked him quickly and swore in a wailing, sorrowing way.

Buck hitched along the bank toward me and offered me his canteen. The chain holding the cap was broken and I fumbled the cap and it rolled down the bank. "Never mind it," Buck said. "Have a drink of Pavuvu water. It makes me homesick to taste that coconut taste."

I took a pull at the warm, coconut-flavored water. Buck must have carried a filled canteen all the way from Pavuvu. It was brackish. "Why didn't you fill it from the bubblers on the transport?" I asked him. "This tastes lousy."

"Be glad you can taste it at all," he told me. "I was sure I was going to get it that time. I woulda sworn it was my time then."

"You always feel that way," John said. "Let's check the line." They sent me out to the right flank of the line. In most places I could walk without crouching. The firing had died down on both sides, except for the artillery that still droned over from ridges to beach and from beach to ridges. Wounded were being carried in from the forward rifle pits on the airstrip. One loudmouthed F company rifleman hobbled by with a smashed leg.

"I got mine," he yelled at me. "How you doing?"

"You aren't off the beach yet," I reminded him.

I passed Joey, the Massachusetts rifleman, who was squatting in his hole with only the top of his head showing. I called to him. I was glad to see he had made it. He said: "I didn't like that at all. I couldn't move out of this hole."

Back behind the bank, a tank driver was hanging out of the turret, arguing with an infantryman about who had credit for the kill of a Japanese tank. Similar arguments, begun before the firing had really stopped, would go on for years at reunions and parties. Wherever Marines gathered there would be arguments about who did what. The Marines were good combat men, but they were never modest or shy about claiming full credit. Army men claim that the Marines had one publicity man in each squad,

and this was partly true, except that the men were unpaid
volunteers who did publicity work on the side; and, unlike
most publicity men, Marines believe their own stories.
One wag and storyteller named Milt, who served in the
Intelligence section, used to say: "Naturally, I believe this
story. I made it up myself."

I found Dannie, our scout in the right flank company,
a very shaken Marine. One of the Japanese tanks had
driven right over his hole while he was crouched down in
it. Dannie gave one of the few eyewitness accounts of what
it was like to be run over by an enemy tank. "It was black
and noisy. I just hoped I wouldn't hit my head on the
bottom of it."

After I put in the flank boundary I went back to the
Battalion CP and we studied the map. Our objectives had
been drawn in as phase lines. The beach was Phase 0-1,
the airport 0-2, the ridges 0-3 or 0-4. We were supposed
to pass all the phase lines and secure the island in three
days.

"Think we'll do it?" I asked Milt. He kept the battalion journal, and he was as close as we came to having a
military expert.

"You want the truth?" he asked.

"As close as you can manage to get to it," I told him.
"What do you predict? The general says three days—short
and sweet."

Milt said: "I don't think it's going to be short. I don't
think it's going to be sweet. And I doing think we're going
to be on Phase Line 4 tomorrow, or the day after tomorrow. This is going to be rough." He looked at all the men
in the CP who were listening to him. "You may quote me
on that. I, Milton the prophet, have spoken. I say this to
all of you: Don't trade off your extra socks for souvenirs.
It's going to be a long and dirty business."

Milton happened to be right on that prediction and
he never allowed anybody to forget it, ever afterwards.

By late afternoon I had toured the line and we had
accurate estimates of our losses in the atack. Our losses
were small compared to the punishment we had dealt out.

There were at least three wrecked Japanese tanks in our area and others further out on the airport and further along the line. Most of the foot-soldiers who followed the tanks had been cut down, or driven back, but there were not a great many Japanese dead lying around. This was true of most of the campaign at Peleliu. Most of the Japanese dead were sealed up in bunkers and caves or buried at night by their mates so that the Marines could not get an accurate estimate of enemy strength. This bothered one old rifleman, and he told me: "I like to see them stacked up like cordwood. Then you get the feeling you've done something."

This was usual for Marines. They hated to take punishment without giving it back, and at that time there was great hatred for the Japanese among the men of the First.

After the attack, we made a search for Japanese prisoners, but none were taken. This seems stupid in view of how little good information we had on the island; but that again was typical. We fought a no-quarter war. I can never remember even thinking about giving myself up as a prisoner.

As dusk came on, we dug shelves against the side of the bank and piled coral chunks up at our back to ward off the backlash of mortar fragments. "They'll throw a few rounds in all during the night," Buck said. He handed me four hand grenades. "Put 'em just under the top of your firing spot. Don't use 'em unless you have to, but use 'em before you fire your rifle. There's some of our boys out ahead."

We finished digging our positions at dusk and went down to the foot of the bank to make coffee. We were dug in almost in the center of the Second Battalion front, and about fifteen yards behind the most forward of our riflemen.

The sky out behind the coconut grove near the beach began to streak, at first with fiery red and then with deep green striated with purple, I sipped my coffee and watched it change colors. For all the vast amount of fire that had been put down on Peleliu, the sky was little changed. During the day it had been dirty with smoke and the black specks of shellbursts, but by nightfall when the planes left it, the sky turned clean again. Like the ocean, the sky could not be dirtied by man for long.

As dusk deepened I felt twinges of nervousness, but Buck, who had shown no sign of fear from the first shot, showed even more nervousness. He could not squat down and sip his coffee. He kept popping up and striding around our small fire. Each time he jiggled up he spilled coffee on his dungarees. As soon as he was up he would catch himself pacing and sit down again. John watched him without speaking. If John felt any nervousness he didn't show it, but it was never easy to know how John felt about anything.

George, one of our OP scouts, sat at our fire and, noticing Buck, he said: "The night has to come, Buck. It has to come on before it can pass."

Buck ignored George. "I hate these nights," Buck said. "You can't move and you can't see and you can't do anything. And I don't sleep when those flares are popping." He kicked coral at the fire. "Rotten, stinkin' nights," he muttered.

"I like the nights," George said.

"That's because you're stupid," Buck told him. "Stupid people don't worry about what they can't see. I knew a guy like you on The Island. Went to sleep when we were out on a patrol, and the Japs dragged him away and used him for bayonet practice."

The Marines always called Guadalcanal "The Island." And they always had a story of something that had happened there. Everything had happened on The Island, to hear the old men talk.

Buck wanted to organize watches, but John was against it. "The Japs have had as tough a day as we have," John argued. "They won't do any more than send in a few infiltraters to bother us."

"It only takes one," Buck said grimly.

"Let the kids out front take care of them. They have to stand watches. We might as well sleep."

"You sleep. I'm going to pull watch."

Dusk had come and visibility was closed down to a

few dozen feet. The smoke, settling in the hollows behind the bank, helped to make it darker. I was sitting against the bank, listening to two machine-gunners argue about where to place a concertina, the collapsible net of barbed wire they placed in front of their guns at night. Their voices came to me loud and clear through the sporadic shellfire and the picky bursts of small arms. One, exasperated, said to the other: "Listen, you lousy replacement, I was stringing doublestrand wire on The Island when you were still in boot camp. Don't tell me how to put up wire, Boot. I know wire, see."

Silence. The argument had ended. "The "elder" man had "pulled his combat time," and this was the way many arguments ended, even arguments about religion and politics, and not about the war at all.

Buck reached over and tapped my arm. He pointed into the gloaming behind us. "Who in blazes are those guys?" he asked. Down along a path near the swamp pond came a file of dark-faced men in Marine dungarees. They were tall and rugged-looking men, and their faces couldn't be distinguished in the darkness that was coming on. They were the first Negro Marines I had seen in the war. They were carrying water and ammunition in from the beach, led by a huge sergeant who carried a box of ammunition on each shoulder. They dumped their supplies at the foot of the bank, and just as they did the Japanese fired a twilight salvo in on the line and everybody scattered for their holes. One of the carriers dived into a hollow between Buck and me, and the three of us lay there while the Japs larruped the line with every gun they had. The dirt of the bank began to slide down, and I turned my face from it and looked into the white eyeballs of the carrier who was right beside me. I heard him say, "Man, man, this is no good. This is real bad."

The barrage began to let up and darkness was full down on the line. The carrier sat up and said: "Where they at? My party, I mean."

"Scattered all over the place," Buck said. "You better not move now."

"This hole taken?" the carrier asked.

"You got it," Buck told him. "There won't be any more heavy fire now because we'd spot their flashes. But it would be very dangerous to move."

"I'm staying right here," the carrier said. "Right in this nice place here."

It was completely dark. I couldn't even see the carrier's white eyeballs. Something popped overhead and everything lit up in a weird shade of green. The ships of the line had started to fire night flares. More flares popped, thrown up by the mortars behind us. They were green, too, the most frightening shade of green I had ever seen. When I turned toward the carrier he looked like a character out of a horror movie, and I must have looked as bad to him because he gasped and said: "Man, that doesn't make you look good at all. I knew people came black and white but I never expected to see any green ones." He rolled over and said to Buck: "What you think I ought to do? I don't hear my people nowhere abouts."

"Do what you want," Buck said, "but if I was you I'd stay right here until morning. You can't do any carrying now dark has come. Everything shuts down."

"Reckon I better stay," the carrier said. "You mind?"

"Glad to have you," Buck said. "You can take the second watch. I'll wake you."

From somewhere in the darkness John laughed. "You can't stop Buck," he said. "If he can't fill his watch list, he recruits guys. Put me down for last watch."

I remember very little of the details of the night. Buck must have stayed awake through all the watches. He never could seem to sleep well on the line. Not that anyone did. Every time a flare broke or a shell rumbled in close I almost choked on my own heart. The line at night has its own curious pattern of sound. There are long lulls when even the small-arms fire dies. When this happens and darkness is all around, the war is far away and you drop off into exhausted sleep. But then comes one shot, sometimes ours, sometimes theirs. A spatter of fire follows, at first rifle fire and then a few bursts from a BAR, and finally the full clatter of a machine gun. Then there is furious exchange as both sides wake up and hammer away in anger. Men call all along the line and flares pop and the shadows rush across the front of the line until you swear that the enemy is attacking in force. Tracers go pumping out into the dark. The mortar men wake and begin to fire a few. The artillery is called down, and the war is on. Then there is a lull, a few embarrassed rounds are fired, and things settle. Sometimes the harsh cry for the corpsman goes up and men ask along the line: "Who got hit? Who was it?"

"Just a guy in the machine guns," a rifleman tells another.

"Just a rifle guy in the first platoon," a machine-gunner tells another.

I woke up many times as short fire-fights flared up. I lay and listened to the fire from both sides. It was easy to pick out the different weapons, just as the different instruments in a symphony orchestra can be identified. It was easy to tell their weapons from ours. Their rifles had a lighter sound and a higher crack. Their machine guns fired faster than ours. Their artillery was more wobbly in flight than ours.

Despite the sounds and the endless, nervous conversation of Buck and the carrier, I managed to fall asleep.

Some time in the night I felt a hand that seemed to be tearing away my shoulder to get at my throat. I had curled up asleep in a ball and when the hand fell on me I unwound and reared up with my rifle pushed out in front of me and my knife in the other hand.

A voice behind the hand said: "Sorry to scare you, man. I tried yellin' but I couldn't make no headway against this other noise around here."

I recognized the carrier's voice and relaxed. It was my turn to go on watch. I rubbed my shoulder. "You got strong hands," I told him. "I think you ripped the arm right off my shoulder."

"Jes' nervous," he said. "Hope I didn't hurt you."

"All quiet?" I asked.

"Never quiet. But we're still livin'."

"I got the duty," I told him. "Relax and go to sleep."

I rolled over on my stomach and faced out toward the airport. I could see our front line foxholes but nobody moved out there. When the flares came up the view was stark and bleak, and when they died everything seemed to move in the running shadows. For a moment I had the feeling that everybody out in front of me had been killed. I turned back from the airport view and it was comforting to hear Buck and the carrier having a low-voiced conversation about automobiles. I called: "John . . . John." But there was no answer.

"He's asleep," Buck told me.

"How's he do that?" the carrier wondered.

"I'd like to know myself," Buck said.

I turned back to watch the airport. Suddenly, during a lull, a voice called out: "Amelicans. Amelicans. Pigs . . . Dogs . . . Amelican pigs and dogs." The voice must have come through a megaphone or a bullhorn. It was louder than life. I jumped and almost opened fire.

"That's a Jap," Buck said. "Some stinkin' miserable clown is crawling around out there. Don't fire. That's what he wants."

"Amelican pig," came the voice. "You die. You die. You die."

Just as the line had opened up to answer rifle fire, they opened up to answer the infiltrater, wherever he was. The language that volleyed out of the seemingly deserted foxholes almost lit the sky. Buck listened to it and chuckled. It was the first time he had relaxed since nightfall.

"They won't out-yell those guys," Buck said. "Nobody could."

"Hey, Shambo," some rifleman called. "Come on in and see what we did to your tanks. We're using them to pack fish in."

"Drop dead, you lousy Jap," someone said, "and save us the trouble of knocking you off."

Worse things followed, some in simple English and some in Japanese. One of the machine-gunners had been born in Japan and he was busy furnishing bad words in Japanese.

"Hey, Tom," someone called. "How do you say '——'?"

Tom would furnish the word or its equivalent. Back would go the word to the infiltrater. "Die! Die! Die!" the infiltrater yelled. The infiltrater had learned his English out of a book and he didn't have either a large or lurid vocabulary. He kept repeating "pig" and "dog"—and this was no match for the words that Tom furnished. The exchange lasted a few minutes and then the officers silenced the men. The Japanese used the trick to get a fix on the positions along the line. The whole exchange ended in a burst of rifle and machine-gun fire.

"I never knew they was so close," the carrier said to Buck.

"Usually they send out a more insulting guy," Buck said. "Some of them, especially the ones born in the States, can really bait you. That one didn't have the vocabulary."

Things quieted down except for a big fire-fight that flamed up over in the third battalion area. My watch was over and I woke John. I just had to touch his shoulder and he was awake and mumbling. I lay back down and tried to sleep, and a burst of fire came from the swamp behind us. That brought everyone awake and everyone was calling to everyone else. We grabbed our weapons and faced toward the rear and waited. The word was passed along the line. "It wasn't any Jap. Some kid cracked up and began to run around. Somebody shot him."

I lay back down again and tried to sleep. I was almost asleep when a terrible call sounded above even the sound of small-arms fire. The scream started high, went higher, gurgled and then rattled and then died. It brought every one of us awake, and the carrier muttered "Lord, lord, lord."

"Relax," John said, "it's only The Screamer back in the CP." The Screamer was a man who had terrible nightmares and who had been having them and screaming his way through them for three campaigns.

"Someday he'll get shot," Buck said. "I mean some night. The guy would drive you crazy if you didn't know about it."

"Go to sleep," John said. "I got the watch."

Finally I did sleep, fitfully, until just before dawn when the first heavy salvos came in with the new light. "Morning call," John said. "Wake, greet the new day, but don't get up or you'll get your block knocked off."

That morning we got ready to attack across the airport. The rations, water and ammunition that the carriers brought up, were doled out to the men. Orders were passed and a barrage was laid down on the other side of the airstrip. The riflemen got ready in their holes.

At the bottom of the bank we built a quick fire, using an explosive they called "Composition C," and put coffee water on to boil. "We'll go out in about fifteen minutes," Buck said. He used his knife in the handle-slit to lift the canteen cup from the fire. He laid out our cups and one for the carrier and made four equal portions of coffee. The carrier said: "I liked you boys fine. But I'm not sorry that I get off here."

"I don't blame you," Buck said. "This attack is going across ground with no cover at all." He looked up toward the ridges where the naval guns were clawing away with fiery hands.

Overhead an air strike came screaming in, bombing and rocketing and dropping fire. The preparation for the attack had started. The tremors from the hills rolled all the way back to the ground where we sat. We could feel the shock in the seat of our pants. The whole island was wriggling.

The Japanese began to answer our fire, trying to jab our attack off balance. We scattered back to our holes to wait. Instead of Buck being pessimistic, John was. He said: "We jump off over about three hundred yards of open ground. Directly ahead are the pillboxes and the blockhouses. Above there are hills full of caves full of Japs and guns. May God have mercy on us. The Japs aren't going to . . ." He touched my arm. "Well, here we go."

Buck stood up and walked over the top of the bank and waved his hand ahead. "Just walk ahead as far as you can," he told me. "Let's move out!"

4

MAKING THE ATTACK

We attacked into a wind blowing down from the scalded hills and over the smoldering and ruined blockhouses; that wind touched our cheeks and it was like the breath from the open hearth of a great furnace. As we moved, just behind the assault companies, the airport clouded over with dust and smoke and wriggling waves of heat. Beneath the arms of the riflemen appeared half-moons of dark sweat, and just below their packs their dungarees showed dark and sometimes white from the salt. It was going to be a very hot day. Already sweat fretted in the open wound on my forehead, and my eyes blurred and stung, and the smell of powder and dust and burning things was everywhere mixed. There was also that peculiar odor that came from fetid pillboxes in which the Japanese lived and died. Buck called it "the stink of death." Perhaps it was.

We were maintaining a floating Observation Post just behind the assault companies, and our contact runner was the pudgy German named Larry, who looked too fat to run; but he could run very well. He seemed too baby-faced to be a combat man; but he was without fear. The only sign of stress he showed was in his face that flushed redder and redder as things got bad. And they got bad.

At first we walked into the humming mist, and ahead of us moved the long skirmish line of riflemen, scything forward all the way to the Fifth Marine lines. The line

ambled, then quick-stepped, then trotted, then drove into
the smoke, running hard. Before them, the shelling built a
wall of spurting earth and flaming explosion and vicious,
whirring shrapnel. Gaps opened in the line. Men bunched
up and then spread out; and finally one long segment of
the line folded down, as the riflemen went to the ground
and returned fire on the pillboxes. A howling series of
shellfire came in, and there was no longer any line at
all—only broken bodies and a few men wriggling ahead on
their own, without orders or control.

We dived into a shellhole and lay still, timing the
mortars which walked all around us. I lay next to John.
Larry and Buck were farther out. When the shellfire hit
and the ground shimmied, John clamped down hard on his
helmet top to keep the concussion from tearing it away. I
saw him grimace and spit into the dust, and he was turned
toward me, shouting something which was swallowed by the
sound around us. I saw his lips and I could catch his
message. He said: "This is a bad one. This will be a bad
one for me." I had never heard John say such a thing
before, and it frightened me, even though I didn't know
then that he was right.

The fire built and built until my ears refused to
receive more sound, and it was maddening, because even
the ground was not steady. The whole field rocked. All
around came the cry: "Corpsman!" No matter how loud
the sound, that call came through. I felt that the artillery
was trying to shake us loose from the earth itself, and I
sprawled full length and dug into the dirt with my fingers.
I was afraid that if I let go I would slip down into some
tremendous hole. I had always been afraid of falling; I had
always been afraid of caves and mines and the combined
fear of them made me scream. But everything else around
me was screaming and it didn't matter. There was no one
to hear it.

John knelt above me. He shouted something. He
waved toward something off on the right. I couldn't understand him and I had no wish to. I put my head down and
bellowed with the fear I felt. Then I felt fearful pain in my
fingers. The pain made me jerk my fingers free from the

holes I had dug with them, and when the fingers were
free I was up and running, off to the right. I supposed,
later, that John had stamped on my fingers to pull me out
of my panic; but he never spoke of it then, or during the
brief time afterwards he was to live.

I was running. Showers of dirt went up in my face
and I was blinded by flash and dust, but I was running to
the right, the direction John had ordered. Everything else
had closed down on me again and my one thought was to
get to the end of our battalion front and see what had
happened. Men swirled around. I flopped and ran, flopped
and ran, while great trains of artillery poured down and
scrambled the ground under me. I dived into shellholes
and rolled out of them and ran on. The air was thickly
seeded with small-arms fire which meant nothing. At last I
rolled down a bank and into a ditch, and other Marines
were there. A captain, a stranger to me, squatted at the
edge of the ditch and tried to see ahead. Behind him was a
company radioman, set up and ready to transmit. Riflemen
had clustered there.

"I can't see," the captain complained to the radioman
and the riflemen behind him. "I can't see, so how can I
tell? It's coming in from everywhere in the pillbox area.
Tell 'em never mind co-ordinates. Tell 'em just to fire and
fire. For Pete's sake . . . the whole front is a target. Put it
onto them." The radioman cuddled his set under him and
put his mouth close to his speaker, and began his call, but
there was no way to hear what he said in that noise.

I rolled close to a rifleman and shouted. "Is this the
Fifth Marines?"

He was sprawled out on his face and for a moment I
thought he was dead. But he rolled over and I yelled
against his ear. He nodded his head. "It's the First Battalion, Fifth."

"Where does the First Regiment end?" I asked.

He shook his head. I didn't know at first whether it
meant no, or that he couldn't hear me. Finally he said: "I
don't rightly know about the First." He hitched up the
side of the ditch. "Cap'n, where's the First at?"

The question annoyed the captain. "I don't know," he

said desperately. "I don't even know for sure where the Fifth is. We're supposed to be the left-flank company. But it's scrambled. I mean mixed. If we could get the rest of the way over and lie up in those blockhouses there we might get some cover. But out here... Well, let's try. Come on!"

He stood up and waved, and his men crept out after him and disappeared somewhere beyond the flaming curtain that flapped in our faces. I worked back along the line toward center, and already I had learned how to move through the worst of it. Anything can be learned, and when life is the motivation it is learned quickly and well. The infantryman's basic trade is either learned or not learned in a day on the line. To be an expert takes months.

The first Marine I recognized from the Second Battalion, First, was lying in a hole, dead. He had been bowled over on his back from the blast and, in death, he seemed to be posed for a picture with the caption HOW TO LOOK VERY DEAD. Just beyond him were a pair of live Marines, a BAR man and his assistant. They said they were from the Second Battalion, First; and one of them said: "We don't know where the rest of 'em are at. Either ahead or back some."

"We oughta go back," the BAR man said.

"Or ahead maybe," the assistant suggested. "There's no cover at all behind us."

"Whatsa difference?" the BAR man said. They began to wriggle ahead and I followed them. The fire had not slackened. Headfirst we crawled into a hornet's nest, until the BAR man clapped his hand to his thigh and I saw blood welling through his fingers. "I'm hit," he said.

"You hit, Freddie?" his assistant said.

"Yeah, I'm hit. I'm going back if I can get there. You want this?" He pushed the BAR along the ground toward his assistant.

The assistant said: "I guess I'm supposed to take it. You ain't hit bad, are you, Freddie?"

"Naw. Do I look it?" He made a gesture toward the smoke and flames of the blockhouse area. "That's what they can do with this war," he said. He went back, dragging his damaged leg behind him. It must have hurt him, but he looked happy enough for me to envy him.

I lost the assistant—now the BAR—in the smoke somewhere. The texture of the ground under my hands and knees had changed. I could feel it biting, and when I looked down I saw sharp fragments of concrete—I had arrived in the blockhouse area. All the first line of pillboxes had been leveled and the fragments spread like a jagged carpet along the ground. I ran against a torn concrete wall with iron reinforcing rods twisted out on all sides. Against it I rested and wondered if anyone else had come across the airport with me. I felt very lonely; but there was no good in calling out, even if my voice could have carried above the din. Finally, I moved beyond the wall, and there was a lieutenant I knew very well. He and three riflemen were firing over a second low wall. The lieutenant had a BAR which he didn't use very well.

"I'm across," he said. "And these men are. But I don't know about the rest. I think they're lying all around, through here." He waved vaguely. "We got hit real bad on the field . . . squads all ripped up . . . we weren't half across."

Two men slid into our position between the walls and

Light Machine Gun

the lieutenant tried to grab them and place them. They had a light machine gun.

One of the machine-gunners said: "Look, sir, I got to see to fire, and I can't see nothin' in here." The lieutenant nodded. The machine-gunners went over behind a high pile of rubble and pegged their gun down and began to fire.

A sergeant came tumbling in beside the lieutenant. The sergeant wore his chevrons painted in black on his sleeve. "He's bringing it up," the sergeant said. "The stuff is coming."

"Good," the lieutenant said. "We can't move until we cave in that gun-slit. Seen any flame-throwers?"

"None. Only one got across, and that don't work."

The dark dynamiter I had seen in the trench near the beach rolled down into the hole beside the lieutenant. The demolitionist still wore the pack with DANGER stenciled below the skull and crossbones. He was thick and hairy and had a face like an old lion. When he got into the ditch he stretched toward the sun, thrusting his thick arms toward the sky and throwing out his huge chest. I expected to hear him roar. "You got the stuff?" the lieutenant asked. He meant demolitions.

The dynamiter yawned again. Again I expected a lion's roar to come out of his corded throat. "I got it. I throw away my socks and food before I ditch this." He patted his pack. "I got it all made up. You give me a little rifle cover and I stick it right in that Jap's ear." He opened his pack and displayed a shaped charge of plastic explosive, fuzed and set to go. The lieutenant moved away from it. The dynamiter fussed with his bundle, pulling on the fuzes and patting the mold. "Oh, baby," he said. "When this rolls in on him!"

The lieutenant made a motion toward the machine-gunners. "Lay it on that slit." He waved at two riflemen. "Get out and flank that baby." The demolitionist lit the stub of an Italian cigar that was like a piece of black rope.

"Gimme lotsa cover," he said to the riflemen. He patted his big stomach. "Lotsa macaroni to roll in close. I bust 'em."

The lieutenant poked his head over the wall. The riflemen wriggled out to the flanks. The machine-gunners made their chatter. The dynamiter stubbed out his Italian stogie and moved ponderously toward the wall. He stowed the cigar in his pack so it wouldn't be wet by his own sweat. He held the charge in his two hands like a priest making an offering. I moved up beside him and he grinned at me. He was fingering a silver medal on his neck chain. He sweated but otherwise was rock steady. Perhaps he always sweated. He muttered something in Italian—probably a prayer. Then he made a gesture with one hand and said: "Hey, Rocco, gimme a break, hey?"

The lieutenant said. "His ears are in. Go get 'em!" The dynamiter wiggled out from behind the wall and, for a thick-bodied man, he could move on his stomach. He was in close to the pillbox, pushing up his charge and then wriggling back, and all the while the machine-gunners and two BAR men poured fire over him until he was lost in the rock dust they kicked up.

He came out of the dust like a surfacing whale. "Fire in the hole," he said, and pulled the lieutenant and me down behind the wall.

The concussion slammed us against the iron rods and, for an instant, we rode a pitching and bucking world. The dynamiter clenched his fist and shoved it toward the place where the pillbox had been. "Eat dust," he snarled. "Eat that and see how it goes." He nudged me in the ribs. "Pasquale gives it to 'em—right in the old La Bonza!"

He fished the butt of his cigar out of his pack. He lit it and smoked. He had expected to be alive, and he was. The next day he got killed, but by then he had probably finished his cigar.

I was working my way back through the rubble toward the airport, and men were still running both ways on the open field. When I got to the edge of the field I made two starts at running out, but both times I turned back and hugged the side of a pillbox. The field was still swept with fire as the Japanese tried to keep us from sending over reinforcements to hold our line. There were shellbursts all over the field, but men still ran through them. I had only to run back, but I couldn't. I hugged the pillbox wall until my fingers were stiff. Then I let go and clubbed at my legs with my clenched fist. But they were useless. I knew then what "paralyzed with fear" meant. It was something out of a dream. I wanted to run. I couldn't. I wanted to walk and I couldn't.

I crawled. Cut hands and bruised knees and all, I crawled until the great *whoosh* of a mortar came in. I was flipped over by concussion to lie under the clanging of great bells. Then I rolled over and was sick. Then I crawled until I thought I heard another *whoosh*. This time the effect was different. I jumped up and ran. I ran and ran, and only John stopped me on the other side of the airport. He got my collar and pulled me in as though I were a wild horse. Then he smashed me in the face and I calmed down. John was capable of intelligent cruelty when it would accomplish something. He knew just how to kill my kind of panic.

I reported to the colonel who had lost touch with his assault companies on the radios. I showed him on the map and on the ground where we were. I estimated we had the survivors of two companies across the airfield. The colonel called the good news back to Regiment, who relayed it back to Division.

John made me a lemon drink in his canteen cup and Buck lit me a cigarette. Larry came in from his side of the line where things were better because the companies had a narrower strip of field to cross. Larry had spent most of his time carrying in a wounded buddy. He had very little idea where the companies were or how many men were across in his sector. Buck, who had been bringing up tanks, bawled Larry out, but it didn't make any impression on him.

"When a buddy of mine is hit," Larry said, "I'm going to bring him in, and they can jam this war for all I care."

"Stupid," Buck said. "If everybody stopped to pick up the pieces, the war would last forever."

Word came in that two more of our company scouts had been hit. Bob was missing and we believed that he had been blown to bits somewhere on the airfield. This bothered me because he was, or had been back in the rest area, my buddy. I went all along the airport looking for him, and Buck didn't call me "stupid," because Bob was one of the section and Buck had a fierce loyalty to whatever small group he happened to belong. I searched out through the airfield, and each time I turned over the body of a Marine I was ready to cry. I didn't find Bob.

At high noon I was sitting in the lee of a smashed blockhouse, my back against the steaming concrete that seemed ready to crack with the heat. Beside me was a big Polish man with half of his dungarees cut away—his left arm wasn't there at all, and his white chest and shoulders above the stump were beginning to burn under the sun. The stump oozed but did not bleed and he was so strong that he still could speak. He said—and shock and pain could not make him any less the man he was—"Look at that! Not much blood at all. No blood I can see. Maybe just a little."

I had just pulled him in and the shock was so fresh, or the wound so bad, that it had sealed in, and, in truth, it didn't bleed then. I waited with him for a corpsman who never came—at least while he was still alive. The arm never did bleed.

In the afternoon we were still slugging through the ruined blockhouses, but we were swinging to our left and making toward the nearest point of the scalded hills. The forward observer for the naval guns—a madcap lieutenant called "Mac"—and I were working out on the left end of the line, within sight of the first point of the ridges. A lot of men, from time to time, joked in combat, but Mac was one of the few who could keep up the patter no matter how bad the going got. When Mac called down a salvo from the guns out on the ships of the line, he invariably said: "This will stimulate the bidding up in the card room of the Jap Command Post."

Mac insisted that the Japanese general played bridge all through the campaign. As Mac pictured it, the high command sat deep in a cave, huddled over their cards, while the battle raged over their heads. It doesn't sound so

funny now, but at the time and in the place it seemed
hilarious, and Mac could always get a laugh out of me.
When the shelling came in heavy on us, Mac would
wriggle up close to me and shout: "Here it comes. Now
we'll catch it. The artillery commander plays Goren, and
his partner, the Chief of Staff, plays Culbertson. The
partner just bid him out of a slam hand and now the
artillery man is dummy, and boy, will he give it to
us!... Slam, slam, slam!"

We brought Mac out so he could set up his Observation Post, but cautious Buck chose a safe place, and Mac
wanted high ground, no matter how unsafe it was. We
were just behind the assault companies and the fire was
heavy all around.

"I don't care if I have to stand on the shoulders of a
tall Jap," Mac told Buck. "I've got to have a high, clear
spot to see from."

We had flopped down behind a pile of concrete
chunks while Mac and Buck argued it out. The JASCO
(Joint Assault Signal Company) radio man and I listened.
Buck wanted to run left to more cover; Mac wanted to
charge straight through the barrage.

"If we get out beyond this area where they're registered, we might see something," Mac argued. "Too much
dust and smoke flying." That was all that bothered Mac
about the opposition artillery: it made it hard to see. The
shrapnel and explosion meant nothing to him. "I have to
see to do my job, Sergeant."

"You'll see something, all right," Buck agreed grimly.
"You'll see Japs."

"That's what I came out to see," Mac said, and before
we could stop him he was up and running directly into the
barrage.

He ran like a knock-kneed duck. I ran behind him,
and Buck, cursing both of us, followed. The poor radioman
humped along under his set, in the rear. We ran right
through the rubble, across a road, and into a clearing
where the artillery had torn down the palm trees and left a
few standing, shredded off every branch and frond. Running into that same clearing from the opposite side was

half a squad of Japanese riflemen. We saw them just as they saw us, and Mac and I dived into a pile of brush, between two tree trunks. There followed one of the most ridiculous scenes I ever witnessed in combat.

Mac unslung his carbine after a great deal of fussing and found that it wasn't loaded. The two extra clips he carried, in a pocket attached to the stock, had been knocked off while we were running. Mac raised his rifle, clicked it, and said: "Bang, bang. I pass." He turned a sweet grin on me and waited for me to fire John's Tommy gun which I was carrying then. I swung up my weapon and squeezed the trigger. Nothing happened. I squeezed harder, but still there was no action. Then I screamed: "Buck—Buck, my Tommy is jammed." Only a ridiculous remark by Mac saved me from throwing down my useless weapon and running for the rear.

Mac said: "Well, partner, if you don't have the cards you can't play them."

Buck saw no humor in the situation at all. He was convinced Mac was crazy, anyway. Buck was between two trees just behind us, and he opened up with his Tommy gun. The very rapid rip of it came right over our heads.

"Keep down," Buck snarled.

He ripped off another burst. There was no answering fire from the Japanese, also lying in the brush among the felled trees. We waited. We were in the eye of the artillery storm. Our fire went overhead to the ridges, and their fire went overhead into the pillbox area. The little bare wood lot was fairly quiet, and only the whispering overhead kept the war from disappearing altogether.

I began to get panicky. "What if they charge in?" I asked Buck.

"They won't charge. Just lie still and don't talk. They're down in the brush somewhere. They're as scared as we are; maybe more. But don't talk. You sound like a scared kid whistling in the dark. They can sense that."

We lay in the whispering clearing. I didn't believe the Japs were scared. Until I had personal friends among the Japanese after the war, I didn't believe that Japanese even felt fear.

Tommy Gun

Mac and I lay very still. We were quiet. At least I was. He said: "I think they're cutting for the deal. Do you know any bad words in Japanese? At least we could go down doing something nasty in the best Marine tradition."

He picked up a big chunk of coral, and I think he meant to throw it if the Japanese charged us. He was the best forward observer on big guns I ever saw, intelligent and without fear, but outside of his specialty the rest of the war was a mystery to him. I tried my weapon again, but it wouldn't do anything. Then Buck crawled in near us.

"Is the bolt back on your Tommy gun?" he asked. I looked. The bolt was forward. I eased the bolt back so Buck wouldn't hear the noise. Mac winked at me. In my panic I had done a very stupid thing. The Tommy gun does not fire with the bolt forward. I had forgotten that. I stood up and poured a long burst at the Japs ahead.

Buck said: "It's firing O.K. now."

"I got it cleared," I lied. Mac went on grinning, but he never did tell Buck.

We lay still for a few more minutes. Then Buck stood up. Two rifles popped at him and he dived down again and lay there panting.

The three of us lay still some more. It was already late in the day, and I wondered if Buck was going to wait it out until dark came. Going back would be dangerous. We were in front of our own lines, or in a gap between them.

"I'd like to get set up before dark," Mac complained. "I can't hit what I can't see."

"Well, just stand up," Buck told him. "That will settle your problem."

And Mac did. He stood up and, in fact, stood up high on a palm branch. The Jap, who must have been crawling in close to lob a grenade on us, was so startled at the sight of Mac's red face that he stood up himself. He fired at Mac and missed. Buck stood up and fired. Buck rarely missed. The heavy Tommy gun slugs knocked the Jap backwards into the bushes. There was no more firing. We waited.

"Shall we try again?" Mac asked. "I think it's about Dave's turn to be the test target." Buck nodded. Reluctantly, I straightened up and stood with my head and shoulders above the branches. When nothing happened, I showed more of myself. Nothing happened again. I stood clear, balancing on a branch. Nothing happened.

"Let's get out of here," Buck said, "before they sign us up in the Jap Marines."

We turned tail and scooted back through the bushes, across the road and into the rubble area. There Mac found a big pile of rubble on top of the dome of a pillbox. "Here is the spot," he said. "On this mighty rock I will build my Observation Post." But he didn't. In the excitement we had lost the radioman. If Mac did sight targets, he had no way to send them back.

"Let's go home before it gets dark," Buck said.

There was nothing else to do. With Mac urging us, we made a half-search for the radioman, but we didn't find him. As we started in, a platoon from the First Battalion had swung over to close the gap in the lines; they saw us and opened fire. One BAR man poured a full magazine over our heads while Buck lay behind a rock and cursed him. The firing stopped and Buck's terrible language sounded above everything else.

One of the riflemen yelled: "Who are you?"

"We're a mixed lot," Mac called. "We were sent out to find the Japanese golf course and blow up the clubhouse. The mission was successful. There is no clubhouse standing on this island."

One of the officers, who knew Mac, laughed. "Let 'em by, boys. You're liable to meet anything out here."

When we talked to the lieutenant, we learned that a gap had opened up and we had been in it, holding it with sheer stupidity and luck. Mac thought that was a fine joke, but Buck couldn't see it.

Mac said: "Lieutenant, I now turn command of this sector of the line over to you. My men and I will go rearwards forthwith."

"I'm no bloody man of yours," Buck said sourly.

On that second night, we set up near the Battalion Command Post—which was among some low, sandy ridges near the edge of the airfield. The area resembled an old sand pit. It started as a noisy and nervous night. Buck was jumpy, as he always was after dark. Firefights raged all along the line, and green flares were overhead constantly. The Japanese were sifting through the gaps in the barracks area just ahead, and the colonel had ordered an all-round perimeter guard on the Command Post. The battalion scout section was put in holes on the outer edge of the perimeter. Buck and I were in one; the map keeper and Milt, the journal keeper, were in another. John was in a hole by himself. He said he was tired and wanted to sleep.

I drew third watch and, shelling or not, I slept through the early watches. In the middle of the night, Buck's hand came down hard on my shoulder and I awoke to hear firing all around us. Buck was crouched near the top of our hole, and his Tommy gun was unslung and ready for use.

"What is it?" I whispered.

"Beats me," Buck muttered. "They seem to be all around us."

As usual, the minute there was real danger, Buck was perfectly calm and ready. He only worried when things were quiet at night and just before nightfall. I could see tracers shooting through the darkness and in with the small-arms fire came the crack of hand grenades and the whine and sting of their fragmentation.

Then it all stopped and somebody was groaning in the darkness. Milt called to me, and we called the company scouts who were beyond us. Everybody answered—except John. Everybody was yelling at everybody else. The map man said: "I didn't hear anything from John. We better go look." The map man and I crawled out toward the sound of the groaning. It came from the direction where John had been. I was scared for him.

We found John about five yards from his hole, lying on his back. When we held a shielded match close to him we saw that he had been shot many times, so many we couldn't even tell where he was hit worst. While we knelt above him, the groaning stopped and the map man said: "He's dead. Or near it."

Word went around the Command Post that John was dead. Up in the center of the perimeter near the executive officer's hole, somebody began to weep and scream. He screamed and cried and blubbered. The exec yelled at him: "Shut up! Shut up! Your blubbering won't bring him back."

"I killed him," the man blubbered on. "I killed John."

And he had. For some reason, John, "the loner," had grown restless in the night. He had moved out of his hole and the other man had been trigger-happy and he had poured a clip into John, without challenging him, without ever giving him a chance. John, a fine man, who had survived four campaigns and dozens of battles as a rifle squad leader, had been killed by one scared man back in the relative safety of the Battalion Command Post.

It seemed very unfair, one of the millions of sour jokes that happen in a war. Mostly it was caused by the cowardice of the man who fired without challenging John. But it also came from the fact John was a "loner," without any real close buddy or companion. At night, the "loner" must be a very strong man in order to control his own fear, without help from a friend. John was a strong man, but he hadn't been that strong.

I crept back into my hole. Buck said: "I'm too tired and scared to move out of my hole now. But when daylight comes, I'm going to kill that guy. That lousy coward. . . . So help me God, I'm going to give it to him the same way he give it to John. I'll put the whole clip right into him."

I think then Buck began to cry to himself. I know I did.

5

THE BLOODY RIDGES

Old Marines talk of Bloody Nose Ridge as though it were one, but I remember it as a series of crags, ripped bare of all standing vegetation, peeled down to the rotted coral, rolling in smoke, crackling with heat and stinking of wounds and death. In my memory it was always dark up there, even though it must have blazed under the afternoon sun, because the temperature went up over 115°, and men cracked wide open from the heat. It must have been the color of the ridge that made me remember it as always dark—the coral was stained and black, like bad teeth. Or perhaps it was because there was almost always smoke and dust and flying coral in the air. I spent four days and nights up on the ridges and it is difficult to untangle that time and to remember when specific things happened.

We went against the first ridge on the morning after John was killed. I went up with the assault company, across a clearing littered with stumps and coral and the scrap of war, up and down low hillocks and through a draw, and then onto the foot of the ridge. We got part way up the ridge and then the hills opened and fire poured down on our heads. Two riflemen and I were plastered down into a hole and there we lay while the world heaved up all around us. We could do nothing but huddle together in terror. We couldn't go ahead, and nobody told us to do so. We couldn't go back. We were witless and helpless, with nothing to do but lie and take it. We couldn't run and we couldn't fight. Not one of the three of us bothered to fire a shot while we lay there through the morning.

We lay in it. Artillery shrieked. Men shrieked. And small arms whined. Mortars, defective in flight, whimpered overhead, and men whimpered. Every living thing on that hill cried out for something.

"Help, for God's sake, help us!"

"Corpsman! Here! *Corpsman!* Doc, I'm hurt bad."

"Plasma."

"Water."

"Artillery! Get it onto them. Stop them from hitting us like this."

"Air! Air strike! Come over with the air strike."

"Support!"

"Help!"

"*God!*"

In the afternoon Buck and I went out with Lieutenant Mac. He had specifically requested Buck because he enjoyed irritating him. We managed to get almost to the top of the ridge without coming under too much fire. There, Mac spread his map, dry-washed his hands, called his radioman to him and said: "My message is this: At J—that's Jane—and at five o'clock on Jane Space, we will try one round on for size."

The radioman began to chant:

"*Hello, Dancer Charlie Peter. Hello, Dancer Charlie Peter.*"

"*This is Falcon Oboe Peter. This is Falcon Oboe Peter.*"

"*Come in, Dancer Charlie Peter. Come in, Dancer Charlie Peter.*"

"*Over.*"

The radioman was silent as he received the answering call. Then he said:

"*Dancer Charlie Peter.
Dancer Charlie Peter.
I hear you five by five.
I hear you five by five.*

How do you hear me?
How do you hear me?
Over."

The radioman listened and then said:

"Dancer, here's a target.
Dancer, here's a target.
Jane at five o'clock.
Jane at five o'clock.
Fire one. Fire one.
Over."

Mac and I edged up to the ridge line and waited for the first great bird to come howling over. The radioman yelled up to us: "On the way!"

The shell came shrieking over and made a vast flame against a distant hill, beyond a deep draw.

"Lovely," Mac breathed. "Lovely." He called down to his radioman: "Pour it onto Janie."

Shells swished by in a steady stream and the hillside flamed and writhed under the barrage. Mac searched for new targets. "Is that a gun that just stuck its tongue out at Item Three? I do believe it is. We'll get to you, my friend, in due course." He called down the new target and then rubbed his hands together with satisfaction. "Oh, the beauty of high ground! I will never run out of targets."

We ducked down as mortar fire came in over the lip of the ridge.

"Insolence will get you nowhere," Mac chortled. "The Falcon will strike again."

We went on spotting targets and Buck was very good at it. The war went on around us, but we scarcely noticed it. On that hill we were the big guns and the other action was beneath our notice.

We spotted targets all through the afternoon. All around us the riflemen stayed low in their holes, but there was something about calling down the thunder of sixteen-inch guns that made us contemptuous of return fire. We felt no fear and we did not bother to get down when the puny return fire of mortars came in.

The heat was terrible. One big, redheaded man, horribly burned and caked around the face and lips, suddenly reared out of his hole like a wild horse. "I can't go the heat," he bellowed. "I can take the war but not the heat!"

He shook his fist up at the blazing sun above. Two of his mates pounced on him and rode him down to earth, but he was big and strong and he thrashed away from them. There was something bad for everybody on that hillside.

Mac kept spotting targets until it got too dark to see and then he tried to talk Buck into staying out on the line that night. "I want to be here bright and early," Mac said. "Nothing like a few hot sixteen-inch shells right on the breakfast table. Starts the day right for them."

Buck agreed to stay if we would move down to the foot of the ridge behind the Company Command Post. Mac hated to be that far away from the action but he agreed and we dug in just behind the Company Command Post. We had scooped our holes in the coral, spread our ponchos and arranged our weapons for the night when the Japanese counterattacked over the hill. We had to go back to the ridges with Mac.

The first night on the ridges was a night of terror. Mac pulled fire right in on top of us. He even fired behind us. To control the fire of ships miles away and to fire into the dark on the word of an observer who couldn't see the man in the next hole was a job which required complete confidence and courage. Mac had both. There would be a whispered word from the nervous radioman: "Under way, sir."

"All rightee," Mac would say. "Let's see where this one lands."

Buck and I, our knees pressing together and our hands on our heads, would wait, while the big bird came screeching up out of the darkness behind us. Orange flamed out in a star with a hundred points and the smash of the hit was like a blow from a dark fist, as all the ground shook. There was a terrible silence while we waited for the cry for corpsmen to come from our riflemen. But no cry came. Instead a flare popped overhead. In the ghastly light Mac grinned at us. He seemed some terrible Irish "ha'nt" as he said: "Sure, the man who had my job before, poor lad, tried this blessed same thing one night. For the life of me I can't remember what he did wrong exactly. Well, we need not worry at all. It will come to me."

Buck had little sense of humor at best, and no sense of humor at night. He muttered, loud enough for Mac to hear: "That miserable, crazy Mick will kill us all."

Insults, even from enlisted men, never bothered Mac. "Now, now, Sergeant," he cautioned Buck. "I've been on this job almost three days and I've never lost an observer team." To the radioman, he said: "Let's bring that fire in a bit. Where are we?"

Late that night we went back to our holes and Buck was close to collapse. He lay down behind his shallow barricade of splintered wood and coral, got his body down as far as he could get it into the shallow depression we had made in the coral, muttered a few curses on Mac, began to mutter his prayers, and fell dead asleep. It was the first time, that I knew of, that Buck had slept since the landing.

The fourth day got lost in a blaze of heat. Men let the camouflage covers of their helmets down to shade their necks from the sun and to protect them from the sting of rock dust that was everywhere. The riflemen looked like desert soldiers. Dark men grew darker, and light-complexioned men suffered the tortures of broiled faces, cracked lips, and almost sightless eyes. Many men threw away their helmets and wore only the old, soft, floppy fatigue caps of the Army. The round hat was a favorite in the First Division. It could be bent into any shape and serve against the rain or the sun.

There seemed to be no morning to that fourth day. While the sun blazed, we swung to the right of the first ridge, crossed a road that led nowhere, and came up against a sheer cliff. Down from this cliff, steep and studded with caves and holes, came Japanese fire. Only by hugging the base of it could we move. Machine-gunners were set up across the road, and the riflemen were assembled at the base of the cliff. The orders were to take the cliff. It was a stupid order.

While the riflemen were being assembled, the fire landed on E Company machine guns, and their screams came to our ears and wracked our nerves. Buck, who had been hugging the cliff in terror, reacted as he usually did when there was something to be done. He walked out across the road and stood up on a rock while mortars poured down around him. Buck and a sergeant from E Company organized a team of riflemen snipers and they began to pick off the mortar observers who were up on the forward slope of the ridge. They also got a bazooka man to fire into a nest of mortars. Then they called in the company and battalion mortars and the Japanese fire dried

Bazooka

up and died. When it did, Buck ambled back to the protection of the ridge, and, once he was there, he showed fear again. Our companies started up the cliff.

We had lost heavily, ever since the beach, but I had not realized how bad the losses were until our companies moved out on the cliff. Clawing and crawling up the cliff went platoons that were no more than squads, and companies that were no more than large platoons. I counted one platoon. It mustered eighteen men on that push. But they went up.

From the base of the cliff, we could pick out each man and follow him until he got hit, went to ground, or climbed to the top. Not many made the top. As they toiled, caves and gulleys and holes opened up and Japanese dashed out to roll grenades down on them, and sometimes to lock, body to body, in desperate wrestling matches. Knives and bayonets flashed on the hillside. I saw one man bend, straighten, and club and kick at something that attacked his legs like a mad dog. He reached and heaved, and a Japanese soldier came end-over-end down the hill. The machine-gunners yelled encouragement.

As the riflemen climbed higher they grew fewer, until only a handful of men still climbed in the lead squads. These were the pick of the bunch—the few men who would go forward, no matter what was ahead. There were only a few. Of the thousands who land with a division and the hundreds who go up with a company of the line, there are only a few who manage to live and have enough courage to go through anything. They are the bone structure of a fighting outfit. All the rest is so much weight and sometimes merely flab. There aren't more than a few dozen in every thousand men, even in the Marines. They clawed and clubbed and stabbed their way up. The rest of us watched.

Watching them go up, Buck, the old rifleman, said: "Take a look at that sight and remember it. Those are riflemen, boy, and there ain't many like them. I was one once."

I looked up the cliff, but everything had changed. There was no longer anyone in sight. Our men who had gone up were either in holes near the top, dead, or lying out wounded and cooking in the sun. Another wave of riflemen got ready to go up, but before they could move out, heavy fire fell again, tearing apart the command posts and scattering machine-gunners and even dropping in behind the low ridge beyond the road, on the company mortar men. Once more, Buck moved out in it and called targets. This time I went with him, out of shame.

We could see Japanese observers, scurrying around near the top of the ridge line. We put everything we had in on them and Buck even yelled: "I wish that crazy officer was here with his big guns."

Before I could answer, a mortar *whooshed* in and blasted us both from the rock on which we stood. I landed on my feet and ran head-down for the base of the ridge. There, safe under an overhanging ledge, I sat, sobbing with an effort to get my breath. I saw Buck pick himself up, dust himself off, and climb back onto the rock. I sat for ten minutes, and then, ashamed of myself, I went out and relieved Buck. If he knew that I had run, he said nothing about it.

In the afternoon we went out on a long patrol, swinging around the nose of the cliff in a sweep to our right. We still had a few men up on the cliff, but we had learned something. Beyond that cliff was a deep gorge. After fighting up to it, we found ourselves isolated, with no chance to go ahead. So we went around. I went out with Larry and a platoon leader and a dozen men and we got a long way out until we were pinned into a blockhouse by heavy fire from the hills ahead. The lieutenant decided that somebody had to go back and report, and the job fell to Larry and me.

We moved to the steps of the dugout and stood there while the fire thundered down overhead. It was a very tough blockhouse. The roof creaked and mortar and sand sifted down on us, but it didn't breach. We took off out of the blockhouse, running. On the way in, everything happened. We hit a Japanese patrol and were pinned down and chased. Then we were spotted from the ridge and pinned down with mortars. Then our own naval guns made a wall of fire which blocked us off. Probably, Mac was calling those shots. When we hit the naval guns, Larry said: "We best run for it. Good luck to you!"

We ran for it. I got in but I don't remember arriving or reporting. I remember Buck dumping pineapple juice into my mouth from his canteen cup. The fruit juice had been sent in from the ships of the line, and never was there a more welcome gift. Men were dropping from dehydration and sun. Larry and I drew two cans each and I drank myself sick, but after the sun went down I could walk again. I even helped Buck prepare our position for the night.

The next morning I got up and joined the line, which was already moving off to our right along the route we had taken the day before. We got all the way to the bunker before we were stopped by fire from ridges which lay beyond a road and a causeway. The colonel took over the bunker as the Battalion Command Post. Later, the Regimental Command Post moved in. It was the best cover in the area. For me, it was like home. When I ran in from the causeway or the swamps, which were off to our right, the bunker was a welcome sight. Once inside, no matter what was coming in overhead, I felt secure. I knew every chink and crack in that foul and damp tomb, but it was home. It was a domed-roof pillbox, two steps down into the ground, concrete on top, steel reinforced, and concrete inside. It took direct hits until the mortar was all shaken out of the chinks between the blocks. But it held.

We were moved over toward a narrow causeway that ran through the swamp toward the road and the ridges. "Hold here," the lieutenant said.

Up on the causeway a memorable thing happened. A Marine came dashing out along it, moving toward the ridge. He was hit and knocked flat. I remember his muddy fingers stretched toward where we lay. He was clenching and unclenching his hand, either from pain or through some death reflex beyond his control. A second man, unable to stand the pitiful sight of that hand, clambered up on the causeway and drove toward the wounded man. The second man was shot to a skidding stop. He lay on his back, without a twitch. A corpsman, who had seen it, said, "Shove this, I'm gonna get those guys." He rolled up onto the bank, got to his knees and never did stand up. The sniper shot him as he still knelt.

A fourth man, a squat and burly ape of a man with extra long arms, reached up over the edge of the causeway and began to pull the men in. He exposed no more than his long, thick arm, and he must have had phenomenal strength to drag the weight he pulled with one arm. I could see him straining and sweating as he began to tug the first of the wounded men over the edge of the bank. The sniper poured fire in at that thick, hairy arm that seemed to reach up out of the swamp like the tentacle of some hidden monster. Mortars harrumped and clopped into the mud; but the man pulled all three wounded men to safety.

Late in the afternoon, they began to patch the line companies with every able-bodied man they could send up from the rear. In came men from the war-dog platoons, the military police, the Division band, the Division laundry platoon, regimental headquarters men and battalion clerks. I was assigned to take these men, each of them carrying a load of ammunition, out through the swamp and into the lines. Most of them were quiet and good men who were scared but not too scared to do what they were told. But a few of them had never visited the front lines and had no intention of going out there. They felt that the riflemen were a special breed, created to do all the suffering and dying for the Division.

A fat clerk complained to me: "I haven't been trained for this. What good will I do?"

I had neither pity nor sympathy for him. "You'll do fine, Fatty," I told him. "You will probably stop two bullets and save two good men."

That fat clerk hated me long before we got into the swamp. Twice I caught him lagging back and looking for a chance to duck. Both times he had dumped his ammunition so he could run better. He finally did bolt when we got into the high grass, and I never saw him again. At the time I was watching another man who was trying to duck out. He had a good reason, too. He was a heavy winner in the Division poker game. He said his pack was stuffed with thousands of dollars in winnings and he offered me a small piece of his money to let him run to the rear. He wasn't worried about himself as much as he was about the money.

"What if I got hit?" he asked. "Some grave-robbing thief would clean my pack."

"I'll see that they bury it right with you," I promised. "Get those belts of machine gun ammo around your neck and move out."

"I'm a sergeant," he told me.

"That's fine, Sergeant," I said. "I'm a private. Let's go."

We had easy going until we were in the high grass. There it was rough. The men with the belts of machinegun ammunition couldn't run and they couldn't get down. The men carrying rifle ammunition in ponchos had a worse time. Nobody panicked until the first carrier was shot and killed instantly. His partner, carrying the other corner of the poncho, put down his load and howled like a dog, and that noise unnerved everyone in the party. Of the twenty, I got nine men to the lines. Probably, no more than one other man had been hit. The rest either ran back or scattered to hide in holes in the grass. I had no time to flush them out of their cover.

After we got the ammunition out to the line, we couldn't find anybody to take it. Once more the companies were milling around, some men retreating and some attacking, but most of them were just lying there, hoping to get out alive. I dumped my ammunition in a Company Command Post and went back to the bunker. It was like coming home to a house in the suburbs after a hot and hard day in the city.

I spent that last night on the line almost entirely out of the bunker. At dusk, as we were boiling coffee water at the entrance steps, a tremendous fall of artillery came down, and two old machine-gunners—who had transferred into the quartermaster section for safety—were hit and blown down the steps of the bunker. We never did make that coffee. We dragged the wounded men down into the darkened tomb and held matches while a corpsman tried to stop the bleeding. The floor of the bunker was soaked with blood. The salty smell of it was everywhere. When Mac came by looking for an escort out to the line, I was glad to go, and we went out of the Company Command Post.

The remnants of our Second Battalion spent a terrible night up there. But, for the few men up on the higher ridge—mostly from C Company, First Battalion—it was far worse. All through the night we could hear them screaming for illumination or for corpsmen, as the Japs came at them from caves which were all around them on the hillside. Men were hit up there and we could hear them crying and pleading for help, but nobody could help them. The remains of the First and Second Battalion and the Division scout section had been thrown in together, and most of the men were strangers to each other. Two or three men were killed by their own mates that night. Grenades slammed and the stinging sound of the shrapnel came down the hill. The cries of Americans and Japanese were all mixed together. It unstrung even Mac.

"I think we ought to get up there," he told the company commander.

"Stay put," the company commander snarled. "Those are some of my kids catching hell up there. How do you think I feel?" He listened to the whimpering calls from the hills, and his head was down between his knees and he cursed monotonously. But he was right. We would have done them no good. "This will be a long, long night," he said.

"A long night," Mac echoed. "I think I'll say a prayer for those kids. Naval gunfire can't help them, God knows."

Of the sixth and last day on Peleliu, I have no connected memory. Short sequences like bad dreams are all that I can recall.

There was a squat, black-bearded rifleman who spoke with a New Orleans accent. He carried nothing but a rifle

and a bandolier of ammunition. His shirt was black with
sweat and plastered to him, skin tight, and he looked like
a pirate. The colonel was talking to him as he got ready to
lead his squad up the hill.

The rifleman said: "Colonel, we can go up there. We
been up there before. And we'll go on up again until
there's nobody left. But we can't hold that ridge, Colonel.
We can't hold it unless there's more of us, sir. We can't
hold it at all, sir. I mean—"

The colonel turned away without answering. He was
on the verge of exhaustion himself.

I remember, too, an old sergeant with an ugly, Irish
face. Perhaps he was only thirty or so but he looked like a
hundred-year-old dwarf, red-faced, red beard, under-shot
jaw, bandy-legged—a wee and ugly gnome. The advance
had been signaled, and the sergeant stood up on his
twisted legs and waved the men forward toward the hill. A
few men stumbled out of their holes. Some could not
move. At least, they didn't. They leaned on their weapons
and looked sick with dread. The sergeant looked at the
men. He turned away and his face twisted with sudden
grief and tears came down his bearded cheeks. He waved
his hand and rubbed his dirty face with his sleeve.

"Let's get killed up on that high ground there," he
said. "It ain't no good to get it down here." As the men
stumbled out for him, he said, "That's the good lads."

There were few platoon leaders and few sergeants.
The young officers had been hit and the sergeants had
been hit or they had folded, and the "duty" fell on those
who would take it. Rank meant nothing. Privates, who had
something left, led sergeants who didn't have it any more,
but who would follow, even if they wouldn't order other
men to. One big Italian man moved forward, dragging his
blanket, unwilling to part with it, even though it tangled
in his legs. Another man had his head covered with a
poncho, so that only his eyes showed. The eyes were like
those of a small burrowing animal driven to ground and
cornered. A small Jewish man, who carried a company
radio, moved around in a circle. He was determined to
move, but he was too damaged by shock and fatigue to get

his bearings. A scout, who walked near him, pointed him toward the hill and the two of them staggered out.

The whole motley lot—a fighting outfit only in the minds of a few officers in the First Regiment and in the First Division—started up the hill. I have never understood why. Not one of them refused. They were the hard core—the men who couldn't or wouldn't quit. They would go up a thousand blazing hills and through a hundred blasted valleys, as long as their legs would carry them. They were Marine riflemen.

A machine-gunner, a Lithuanian, sat calmly at his gun, alone and beyond the causeway. Fire threw rock dust and powder and shrapnel all around him, but he did not move and he did not even flinch. He made no effort to protect himself. His gun was neatly set and laid in to cover the break in the ridge through which any counterattack would come.

He said to me: "I can't go up that hill again. I got no legs now. But no Japs will come through that hole while I'm here." He was sharp-faced and clean, even in the middle of the barrage. I remember that.

In a swamp, an old sergeant crouched in his hole. He had been away from his outfit for two days and his were the motions of a hunted animal. "I got nothing more inside," he said. "Nothing. I don't even know anybody who is still alive. They're all gone, boy. Done, the whole lash-up."

I never found out what we were doing, tactically, on the sixth day. At first, I did what they told me to do, but no more. I ran around to the jumbled messes that were called companies and I tried to help our colonel keep some control of the scattered survivors of many outfits that made the last push up the ridges. Things started bad and got worse and, finally, hopeless, I quit.

I picked up the rifle of a dead Marine and I went up the hill. I remember no more than a few yards of scarred hillside, blasted white with shellfire and hot to touch. I didn't worry about death any more. I had resigned from the human race. I only wanted to be as far forward as any man when my turn came. My fingers were smashed and burned, but I felt no pain. I crawled and scrambled forward and lay still, without any feeling toward any human thing. In the next hole was a rifleman. He peered at me through red and painful eyes. Then we both looked away. I didn't care about him. He didn't care about me. I thought he was a fool and he probably thought I was the same. We had both resigned from the human club. As a fighting outfit, the First Marine Regiment was finished. We were no longer even human beings. I fired at anything that moved in front of me. Friend or foe. I had no friends. I just wanted to kill.

The history of the First Division says that we were relieved late in the afternoon of the sixth day. I don't remember coming down the hill, but I remember sitting by the roadside, in tears. I don't know why. I hadn't cried at all up on the hill. I suppose I was becoming a human again, after some time away from being one. When you come off the hard places, you crawl on your stomach and then move on your hands and knees and then go forward crouching and, at last, you walk erect, and then you feel like a man and it feels awful. Ever since Peleliu I have wondered if animals in danger feel things keenly. I didn't, the one time I turned into an animal. I didn't even feel the pain in my hands until after I was off the line.

The Division History says that by nightfall on the seventh day the First Marine Regiment reported their casualties—1749 men. That was out of 3500. It seemed as though there were more. The line companies were decimated.

We camped back near the first ridge and ate hot food and read our accumulated mail. Then we moved across the island near Purple Beach and camped in a swamp, and the first night I was on guard a Japanese infiltrater got close in on me and I stood up just as he threw a hand grenade. We saw each other at the same time and I was quicker, or scareder. He knocked me down with the concussion of the grenade, but not before I knocked him flat with the direct burst of a Tommy gun. I took one small piece in the lower part of my back. I would have used it to get off the island, but we were going anyway.

On a dark and rainy day, eighteen days after we landed, we went out through heavy, oily swells and under lowering skies to load onto LSTs and eventually a hospital transport, the *Tryon*. We had had a few days' rest, but some of us had trouble getting up the cargo nets and over the rail with what equipment we still carried. My fingers bothered me still. The back was nothing. I remember the big, thick wrists of the sailor who helped me over the rail, who had looked into our faces and seen what was plainly there. He wanted to be comforting. He said: "You gave it to 'em real good, boys. Good on ya'."

An F Company rifleman heaved himself over onto the deck and, for a moment, he lay there helpless like an overturned bug or turtle. Then he got his legs under himself and stood up and pain showed in his face. He said to the sailor: "No—no, we didn't give it to 'em good. We didn't give it to 'em at all. We got beat." He looked back toward the low-lying island and shook his head, as though he still couldn't believe what had happened there. "We won before. We'll win the next one. But this time we got beat, swabbie.

"And that's the truth of it."

6

REST AREA: THE WAKE ON PAVUVU

In the dead-hot days before the fall rains, the First Marines returned to Pavuvu, and disembarked two abreast into the crowd on the pontoon floats. Behind the docks the sun made a glaring puddle out of the coral parade area: everything went out of focus in that glare. The sun washed the color out of the coconut grove and the mountain and made Pavuvu a pale dream of homecoming. The rest base of Pavuvu wasn't home; but it was safer than where we had been.

The men who had been hit early and flown out of Peleliu waited for the outfit on the docks among the rear echelon and the replacement platoon leaders who had already arrived. We had lost heavily in young officers up in Peleliu, and a fresh batch wearing new khaki and shiny bars waited on the dock. Bob and Artie were there and they looked good because I had never expected to see either of them again. They tugged at Buck and me as we filed past and they called us names to show how glad they were to see us. I saw another man I knew well, but when I started to speak to him I couldn't recall his name. I couldn't even march past him until someone moving up from behind me in the file pushed me and I stumbled along. It was like that in the days right after the campaign. I dreamed. I knew what I should do, but my muscles or my voice failed to do anything.

Buck's voice was in my ear as the squads and compa-

nies formed on the parade. "You see them back there—
George, Artie, Bob? All them guys."

"It's good," I agreed.

"Good!" Buck echoed. "Man, everyone is alive. It's
more than just good."

I said: "Not everyone. John wasn't there. The lieutenant wasn't. Wingy wasn't."

Buck said: "Whatta we care about Wing? That crazy
kid! What's the matter with you?"

"I don't know. Either I can't sleep or I can't wake up.
I don't know which."

"We're all right now," Buck said. "It's made. Unwind."

"I'll be all right after we get the wake over."

I knew that the first night back in rest area was always
bad. The brothers and the buddies and the cousins from
other outfits came by to ask about the wounded and the
dead. I didn't want to go through it. I didn't want to talk
about wounded and dead or even think of them. But I
knew I would have to because it was a duty that those who
had lived had to fulfill. We would have to talk, and say
nice things about the dead, just as old people did at a
wake, back home. Then, afterwards, we'd go out to other
regiments and ask about our own friends. I dreaded that,
too. The whole First Division had been badly hit. I had
two dozen or more friends scattered in other outfits, and I
didn't want to know the score on them.

"If I can get through tonight, I'll be all right," I said.
"When the wake is over."

Buck nodded. "The first night is rough like that," he
agreed.

The column moved across the parade toward the tent
area in the coconut grove, where the amplifier on the
Division movie screen blasted canned march music, and
the wounded ran along beside the file like kids chasing a
street parade. I tried to wake up and get with the celebra-
tion, but I couldn't come out of the cocoon of dreams that
had been around me since the outfit left the lines.

How bad was it in the other outfits? I wondered. The
Fifth and Seventh Regiments were hit almost as hard as

we were. More than half my friends had been riflemen. It would be very bad. We had three killed in the Intelligence section and three badly wounded. That was out of sixteen. All sixteen had been hit. I looked at the men who laughed in the files all around me. Less than a week before some of them had seemed unable ever to look happy again. Now they laughed and cheered and capered along. Men came out of the shadows and into the sun so fast. . . . But I couldn't. I even felt a little angry at those who were celebrating. Why should they ever be able to laugh? Later I realized that some of them were not laughing inside. They laughed aloud out of habit. It was a nervous reaction.

Under the roof of the grove it seemed almost chilly. Color came back into things, a deep green like the bottom of a lagoon or the floor of a rain forest. Some of the enthusiasm was running out of the column now because there were so many tents to fill in the Second Battalion area—and many had forgotten how big the battalion had been before.

We were in our old tent; our packs and rifles were dumped and we were stripping for the shower. Buck held himself stiffly and kept his eyes away from the empty cots. Bob came in. He up-ended a water can and sat on it. He had been hit on the third day and flown out, and he kept some chatter going for a while describing how scared he had been when they strapped him down to his bunk on the evacuation plane.

But then his eyes went around the tent to the empty cots and he said: "Well, I've got some coffee for tonight."

"That's good," Buck said. "Are you going to move in here?"

"Yes," Bob told him. "There seems to be plenty of room."

"There's room all right," I said. "You got the soap, Buck?"

I knotted a big brown towel around my waist and ducked out under the tent flap. I didn't want Bob to start talking about the wounded and the dead before I had a shower. I tried to escape. But I had forgotten to take off my socks. I came back and took my socks off and put my shoes on over my bare feet. I started to say something that didn't come out. Nothing I said or thought seemed to end right. We went out into the company street. It was packed coral sand. Each street ran between two rows of coconut palms but at mid-day there was no shade. Buck shaded his eyes in the glare and complained about "Pavuvu squint." He worried a lot about his eyes because he was a first-class shot. Shooting started me remembering about the lines and I stopped thinking about anything but the shower.

Nobody sang in the shower. The water felt so good against the back of my neck that it made me dizzy and I almost fell against the canvas sides: I had to go outside and sit down. The shower did mean something to me. As it peeled off the layers of grime from the lines and the transport, it took away some of the war. A shower is far better than any meal or any letter or any person's words. It makes an end to war in the best possible way by peeling its dirty covering away.

When we came back to the tent, Bob was gone. Buck lit a cigarette and lay down on his cot. He was still wet from the shower and wearing only a towel across his middle. In the E Company tent row behind us, a handwound phonograph was playing a sad song about April. Buck began to talk very rapidly. It was the way he unwound after action. Before he went into the lines he was sullen, and sometimes ugly, and he prayed alone in the battalion chapel. Afterwards, he ran down, like an overwound alarm clock—just making noise and no real sense, talking and chattering about everything from baseball to automobiles he would like to own.

Bob came back to the tent carrying a blackened can for boiling coffee over an open fire. The old men who had been in Australia called it a "billy can." He started a fire in the pit behind the tent and put water on to boil. Bob was very proud of his coffee-making. He puttered around straightening out the tent and sweeping the floor. He had his own method for unwinding. He kept busy with his housework.

Bob saw me lying on the cot staring at the top of the

tent. He said: "Let's go down and get our books out of company property."

Bob and I had books "borrowed" from libraries all over the Pacific. We kept them in bookshelves that he had made out of packing crates. They were good books and we were proud of them and lent them out and had meetings to talk about them. I don't know whether some of those Marines have ever discussed a book since, but they did on Pavuvu. Sometimes men got angry enough in the discussion to go out and fight in the company street. I dressed and went down to company property and picked up our crates of books. The company property sergeant wasn't supposed to store such things, but he was a member of the book club, too.

When we came back with the books we made lunch. We opened tins of meat and spread it on crackers and drank coffee in our canteen cups. They were serving food at the battalion mess, but it was always bad and there were long lines to wait in. After Peleliu, it wasn't the long lines. It was the short lines. None of us wanted to see how short the mess lines were. So we ate in our tents.

Milt came by with a rumor about a package delivery. Milt always had what the Marines called "the word"—the latest rumor. He helped us unpack the books and arrange them on the shelves. I tried to get interested in the books and in an argument that Milt started, but I couldn't. In the hottest part of the afternoon we rolled the mosquito nets up on the poles of our cots and lay down for a nap.

Afterwards we went for another shower and then made some more coffee. There were days when we took six or seven showers and drank ten or twelve cups of coffee. It helped pass the time. And it did that day. I was surprised when evening came and the day had gone. I couldn't remember what I had done to pass the time. I started two letters, but I couldn't finish either. Worry about the night and the wake and the visiting kept me helpless all afternoon. The older men had been through it, and they just let it come. Many of them had gone on their last campaign and were due to be rotated home. They lay on their cots and thought about that, perhaps. Late in the afternoon a friend of Milt's brought some fresh meat down from the galley. We cut it into thin steaks and cooked it over the fire. We also had a loaf of new bread from the baker, who borrowed our books. You had to swap to live.

We made more coffee. Some new replacements unloaded from transports, but we didn't go out to see them. "I don't want to see them," Buck said. "I don't want to know them."

Most of the new men in the company went to the movies that night, and the Peleliu men stayed in their tents. Bob brought a gas lantern and two tables made of orange crates to the tent. Patsy and Jack, two machine-gunners, came by to get a bridge game going. Milt joined them. I tried, but I couldn't play more than a hand or two. Phil took my place.

The night breeze we called "Angel's Kiss" was in off Macquitti Bay, but it stayed high up in the palm fronds and scarcely moved the tent ropes. I lay on my cot with the netting rolled and watched the company street for the first callers. In E Company someone was trying to play on the harmonica the sad song about April they had played on the hand-wound victrola; The song sounded much more mournful on the harmonica, and futile because the man couldn't get the same chords. Bob tended an oil fire in the pit behind the tent, brewing coffee for the wake.

The first visitor came in with his cap in his hand and stayed in the dark half of the tent. He refused coffee.

"I came about Stash," the visitor told us.

"Stash went out the third day," Buck said. "It was in the bunker area. He was lying beside a flame-thrower, and it exploded somehow."

I said: "Yes—napalm burns."

"Where?" the visitor asked.

"Around the eyes and face." The visitor's hands ridged out with veins as he gripped his cap. "How's Stash going to work blind?" he asked.

Buck said: "All we know is that he got burned around the eyes. Nobody said he was blind." He called toward the back of the tent: "Bob, you hear anything about Stash—

that Pole scout with G Company? He was hit just after you."

Bob came in carrying a canteen cup of coffee. He gave it to the visitor, who forgot that he had refused it the first time. The visitor was muttering in some language, probably Polish. Perhaps he was cursing us. That was his privilege.

Bob said, "I never saw him on the ship. But I heard from a guy who claimed to have seen him on Manus in the hospital. He isn't blind. But he's scarred a little."

The visitor sighed. "Well, never mind. 'Long as he can see. He's married to my little sister."

The visitor drank his coffee. He and Stash were from the same coal town. He talked about it, but he was still upset and ashamed of his English. Maybe the books and the bridge-players embarrassed him. He left. Milt and his friends, the machine-gunners, went on playing bridge under the Coleman lantern.

Two friends of Reb, the E Company scout, came by. Reb hadn't been hit so bad, a few grenade fragments in the shoulder and arms. One of Reb's friends said in his soft Georgia voice: "Ol' Reb got hisself out right enough."

"A few pieces in the shoulder," Bob told him.

Reb's friends were having coffee when Wingy's brother stopped by. I had known he would. Wingy had been killed as an F Company rifleman, but he had been with the scout section until just before Peleliu. Buck had transferred him out because Wingy couldn't read a map, and Buck didn't like him anyway. I was nervous about the visit of Wingy's brother and what he would say.

Wingy's brother, a sergeant of machine-gunners in the Fifth Regiment, said without ever asking: "Wingy got hit bad."

Reb's friends put down their coffee cups and said, "So long," and went out. Nobody said anything to Wingy's brother for a moment. Bob went out and got another cup of coffee and offered it to Wingy's brother.

"He got hit bad," I said at last. "He got hit in the amtrac going in. I thought that finished him. But he got off the hospital ship and came back up when we were at Bloody Nose Ridge."

Buck said: "That's where he got it bad, machine-gunned in the stomach. He was carrying a BAR in F Company. I busted him out of this section and into a rifle outfit. He couldn't read a map very well, and he wanted a lot of action. So it's my fault."

"No, it wasn't," I said. "It didn't make any difference. We were all in it together up on the ridge. So what difference did it make?"

Wingy's brother waved his hand. He sounded annoyed. "It doesn't matter about that. Somebody pushes somebody who pushes somebody. It's like knocking over dominoes. I sent a few men out on bad spots. Wingy get back to the hospital ship?"

Milt put down his cards. "They got him out there. But he had died on the way. I saw the KIA report in battalion records."

Wingy's brother listened, grinding one fist into the palm of his hand and swinging his shoulder as though he were getting ready to punch. Nobody else in the tent said anything. The card game had stopped as a matter of courtesy. The harmonica started playing again in E Company; the man got worse but he never stopped trying to get the tune. The futile sound of it irked Wingy's brother and he yelled at the E Company tents: "Rest with that, willya?"

The sound stopped. Wingy's brother said, "Well . . . well, what can you say about a kid like Wingy? I guess he had plenty of moxie, though, coming back a second time."

"He had plenty of nerve," Buck agreed.

"Plenty," I said. "Wingy didn't lack courage at all."

Wingy's brother finished his coffee. "I'll be over sometime to pick up his personal gear. Any of you good at writing letters?"

"He is," Buck said, pointing at me.

"I wish you'd write one to our mother, about Wingy. Pick out the good . . . Well, you know the kind."

"I'll write it tomorrow," I promised.

Wingy's brother made a face. "That's more than he did. He wouldn't write. Well, you know how he was, just a happy-go-lucky kid." We didn't say anything.

"He'll write a good letter," Buck promised. "And Wingy might get a medal or something."

The brother said: "That medal means nothing to me. It might to my mother."

After Wingy's brother left I didn't mind the wake any more. The worst was over. A friend of John's came by, but he was an older man, and he got the details and left without saying much. I was finally coming out of my dream world, and in my mind I was working up the letter to Wingy's mother. I'd have about half-a-dozen letters to write, but Wingy was a special problem. I felt sorry for his mother and I was going to write a long one and a good one.

Finally, Buck said: "We've had it for this night. Let's shove off."

We went into other outfits to ask about our friends. We drank coffee and listened to good news and sometimes to bad. We acted angry at the men who gave us the bad news, and they took it just as we had. Somebody had to be blamed, and it felt good to feel angry rather than guilty.

When we came back from visiting we went to the Battalion Chapel down across the softball field. We all went inside and knelt between coconut log benches up near the altar. The chapel wasn't jammed, but there were a dozen or more men in the darkness, praying. Two down near the back were smoking. It was open on all four sides and had a thatched roof, so the smoking didn't seem so bad. I made it through a prayer. It wasn't much of a prayer, but it was the first thing I had managed to end since I came off the lines.

The next morning they moved one of the new replacements in with us. He was a noisy kid who spent a lot of time sharpening his knife and telling us how many Japs he would kill in the next campaign. He got on Bob's nerves. He seemed so noisy, perhaps because we were so quiet after coming back from the lines. Buck put him on mess duty to get him out of the tent.

"You're going pot-walloping," Buck told the kid. "Just use that same circular motion you use on your knife and whetstone. You'll be the best pot-walloper in the Division.

Maybe they'll let you slice meat or something up there."

In the next few days Buck and Bob and the other old men found the noise of the new men more and more nerve-racking. Bob decided he wouldn't get out of his cot any more. He and a mortar man named Artie had a contest to see who could stay longest without leaving his cot. We carried food to the contestants, and everybody came around to see them from all over the Second Battalion. It was called "the Battle of the Sacks." By the rules, a man could be out of his cot no more than two minutes. Bob finally won because there was a good movie down at Division Headquarters and Artie couldn't resist seeing it. The contest lasted two days. It was silly, but it took our minds off the war awhile, and anything that could do that was important.

7

THE PACIFIC PARADISE

On the fourth day after we had returned to Pavuvu, a call came for a volunteer scout team to man submarine watch on an outlying island. The duty was for ten days. Buck volunteered for himself, Phil, George, Ralph and me.

"We'll get away from the noise here," Buck said. "We can fish and hunt and swim and nobody will bother us. This will be the best duty you ever had."

We weren't so sure about Buck's scheme, but we went along with it for the food, if for nothing else. They gave us our pick of canned stores at the battalion galley. The cook baked extra loaves of bread for us and wrapped up some steaks and a huge chunk of bacon. We loaded our food and weapons on a Higgins boat and set out that same afternoon. We were going out to the best ten days of my war, but I didn't know it until I saw the post.

The post was on a point of land covering a channel between two islands. On our side of the channel were white beach and coconut groves growing right down to the water. About fifty yards inland was a high coral bluff with more groves. On the other side of the channel was a thick rain forest and a tangled mass of fern and liana vine growing down to the water, and mangrove that grew out into the channel itself. The channel was not wide. We could throw chunks of coral almost across it. For the outpost squad, they had put up a pyramidal tent on a wooden floor and frame, and it was just in from the beach, among stunted coconut palms that had their many legs stuck into the sand. There was a breeze coming down the slot and off the water, shade from the palms, no mosquitoes and little heat.

As we went inshore in the Higgins boat, Buck said: "I scounted this place months ago. Think I'd volunteer for anything but the best?"

I remember the ten days on "subpost" as I remember summer vacations when I was very young. They were the fullest, longest-shortest days I ever spent. It was another one of those islands of calm in the middle of war that men like to remember to balance out the other things.

One day was pretty much like the rest. We woke early, not because we had to, but because the sun came to us early along the channel. Waking, I could watch channel light moving in silver swirls on the tent ceiling. Phil, already up, had started a fire in the coral block fireplace. Coffee was on, Phil liked to make an early pot of coffee and serve us a canteen cup while we still lay in our cots. We drank our coffee, smoked and planned the day, while lying in the morning cool that came in off the channel. It wasn't a breeze, but rather one long draught of sea-clean air.

"I think we ought to go on patrol down to the plantation house," Buck said. "Everyone agreeable?"

"You're the boss, Sergeant," George said. "Meanwhile, let's go for a swim."

While Phil opened tins of fruit, mixed pancake batter, and laid out strips of bacon, we went down to our private beach—seventy yards of white sand, deeper and purer than the kind that is spread on Waikiki behind the Royal Hawaiian Hotel. The bottom of the channel was clear sand all the way across to where the mangrove started underwater. We lazed in the sand or swam out and floated in the clear channel water. There were both sharks and barracuda, but we were never bothered. There were crocodiles sunning themselves on a sand spit in a river beyond the mangrove on the opposite shore. They didn't bother us and we didn't bother them. Over the water skimmed white cockatoos and green, blue and red parakeets. We squirted water up at them. They buzzed us, cawing up a ruckus, and then went on to roost in the coconut palms.

Phil was a farm boy who didn't like to swim in the ocean. When breakfast was ready he called us: "Chowdown, you lazy tramps!"

Breakfast was our biggest meal. When our bread ran out we made pancakes, one big one to a pan. We used two pots of coffee at breakfast. We cooked bacon for breakfast and a little extra for our sandwiches, which we made out of pancakes or bread. We had two or three kinds of jam, tinned fruit, and sometimes fresh oranges or bananas and limes. We had powdered eggs and even a kind of root, like potatoes, that we dug from the garden of a deserted plantation. We ate well.

About nine o'clock we took our rifles, a pack of lunch, and canteens full of sugared lime water, and went out on patrol. We were supposed to be looking for submarines that might be sneaking through the back channel on to the Division Headquarters. But we didn't waste time looking for submarines. We had sounded the channel and found that it was too shallow for anything but a torpedo boat. Even if we had seen a submarine we could not have reported it. Our phone line to Division was out and we never had it fixed all the time we were on outpost. So we didn't bother to look for submarines. That part of the Pacific was peaceful in those days. The Japanese had been driven north or were cut off and "dying on the vine" in a few isolated islands.

We worked up the beach early in the morning and, at a small river which cut a hundred tiny channels through the sand to the sea, we halted, had a drink of lime water and a cigarette. We sprawled in the sun, letting the rising heat work through our muscles and bones, while the breeze coming down the slot cooled our foreheads.

"Shall we give Old Snouts a chow call?" Phil asked. Old Snouts was our pet crocodile who lived in that river.

"Why not?" Buck said. "He'll get too fat if we don't give him some ducking practice." We sneaked up the little river and crawled in behind some drifted stumps. Buck kept watch. When he waved his hand we knew that Old Snouts had poked his nose above water. Silently we raised all five of our rifles, the four M-1's and the one carbine which Phil carried.

"Is he going up on the sand?" Ralph asked.

Buck shook his head. "The old bum is too wise for that. But I think he's pulling into the shallows. Steady fire now."

As soon as Buck sighted the dark bulk of the crocodile in the shallows he dropped his raised arm. We cut loose with all the weapons we had. Sometimes Old Snouts would go flopping out of the shallows as he drove for the deep, dark water. We didn't particularly want to hit him. In fact, the game was to miss him, but close. George described the game best when he said: "This is an experiment to see if a crocodile can get combat fatigue. Just imagine a cracked-up crocodile!"

After we had hunted further up the river, we crossed it and went along the beach to the copra docks of the plantation. The Japanese had driven the growers out about two years before, but the warehouses were still full of the rotten, sweet smell of copra. A long jetty ran out from the warehouse, and we dived off the end of the coral blocks and splashed around, having our second swim of the day. The jetty had been made big enough to berth some fair-sized coasters and copra boats. Probably, in its day, it had seen some rough characters put into the port; men like Bully Hayes, the slaver and pirate who worked the Pacific Islands. No boats used the jetty in our time, except for our own boat. We found an old dory, and I found some

M1 Carbine

oakum and tar in the warehouse and we patched it up and made it seaworthy. We used the dory to scull past patches of mangrove where it was too difficult to walk and too dangerous to swim.

Sometime around noon we went up to the plantation house for lunch. By agreement, we let all our watches run down when we came to the outpost. We kept track only of the days. Phil said: "This may be the only time in our lives when we won't have to know the time of day. The heck with watches. We live by the sun." And we did.

The plantation house was a standard affair in that part of the Pacific; it belonged to the Burns Philp chain that grew copra for soap and chemical products. The house itself was frame, painted yellow, with a corrugated tin roof painted brick-red. From a distance the roof looked like tile, but it was tin. We opened up the house but it was musty, and we preferred to lunch in the front yard, under the shade of lime trees, pepper bushes, and a persimmon tree. At our backs was a low wall, dripping with bougainvillaea. Our lunch was sandwiches, fruit and coffee.

After lunch Buck and I napped; Phil, George and Ralph played hearts with our one battered pack of cards. Sometimes we played a few hands of bridge, but usually that was a night game.

About two I woke and Ralph said: "Let's get back to the ranch." We cut along the high coral spine that ran the length of the grove and ended behind our tent. The "high grove" was full of wild steers—scrub beef with long horns and stringy flanks—as fearless and wild as African buffalo. The plantation men had driven them out when the Japanese invaded the area. In the groves the cattle had thrived and the young bulls were kings of the island, until we came along. The grove was still not overrun by the jungle, so the feed was good among the coconut trees. The first bull we sighted gave Buck a terrible fright. We were cutting through the grove and Buck and a gray bull met eye-to-eye near a coconut tree. The bull snorted and hooked at Buck, who dodged behind the coconut tree and hollered: "Hey, there's some kind of wild animal in here that looks as big as a buffalo."

"Where is it?" Phil asked.

"Right on the other side of a tree from me. Get me out of here."

We began to circle whatever it was that had Buck hiding behind a tree. We got all around the quarry, and then Phil said: "Hey, wait a minute! That's no wild animal. That's nothing but a longhorn bull." With that, Phil fired in the air and the bull dashed into the bushes after him. Phil hid until the bull went away.

Buck, who did not like to be bullied by man or beast, growled, "We'll have some fresh meat before we leave this island."

Late in the afternoon we patrolled through the grove on the bluff above our tent. There we shot for giant tree lizards. Those things looked like prehistoric monsters— five or six feet long, and quick as a snake. We ran them into trees, but we never hit them. There were only two of them on the island and we didn't want to kill off our sport.

Buck had heard that they were helpful in keeping down insects. "Never kill off a useful thing," he said. "Ugly as that baby looks, it catches a lot of flies and mosquitoes."

George said: "It looks big enough to eat people."

Buck had no feeling for the beautiful white cockatoos and parakeets; he shot a few of them for the tailfeathers. George and Ralph and I never had the heart to shoot the birds. They were too beautiful on the wing. When they went through the green fronds in a great shower of white, or when they skimmed and dipped over the channel with sun on their plumage, it took harder men than we were to shoot them.

George told Buck the day he shot the first one: "I could never do that."

"Why not?" Buck asked. "I can use the feathers for my hat. There's plenty of them and they don't do anybody any good. Besides, they're noisy."

But Buck shot only one more, although he pretended to be firing at many of them. When he really aimed he did not miss. He didn't want George to know that the beauty of the birds had any effect on him. So he shot at them and missed.

When we came back to our tent, we cut down green coconuts and drank the sharp milk from them. George was our climber. He could go up a tree with his hands and bare feet, just as the natives did.

We used George's climbing agility in our antisubmarine game. We played this late in the day, when it had cooled and we felt like running. Buck gave the signal. Our roles in the game were fixed:

First George scooted up a tree down near the edge of the beach; he hung out from the lower branches and peered seaward and yelled in a voice loud enough to start the birds flying: "Jap pig boat. Sub in the channel. Get 'em, men!"

Buck raced out onto the beach, wearing a towel around his middle and high mosquito boots. The towel flapped and the boots flopped as he ran, and Buck made an effort to look as ridiculous as he could. Pointing out to sea, Buck yelled: "You there in the pig boat! I have you under observation."

While Buck held the imaginary boat motionless in the channel, Phil, Ralph and I grabbed our weapons and raced for the top of the bluff. When we were in position, Buck yelled: "Give it to 'em, men!" At once we began to yell: "Bang! Bang!" The first time, we actually opened fire—but one short round almost killed Buck on the beach, and after that we "simulated" the firing by yelling, "Bang, bang!"

George called out the score while we fired. "Direct hit on the periscope. . . . Right up the old torpedo tube. . . . Through the conning tower and out again. . . . You got the skipper, right through the backside. He's bleeding gold braid."

"Cease fire," Buck ordered us, "while they remove the dead and wounded. I think they're going to surrender and strike their colors. Yep, there comes the flag down. Holy mackerel! That's the American flag. Men, we got another one of ours."

From the tree George protested: "It still counts. It still counts. Mark it up! That's why those submarine guys get the extra pay—for dangerous work. Mark up another one for us. Nobody told us not to shoot our own."

The game ended when Buck drew a picture of a submarine in the sand. That was the way we tallied our "kills." Each day the tide came in and washed away our score, and so we never got more than one to our credit. When I think back on it, Marines played games as little boys the world over play them.

In the evening we had our third swim of the day. We stayed down on the beach until Phil called us in for supper. If we met natives during the day, we got fresh fish for supper. We traded off cans of corned beef for the fish, but after a while the natives got sick of corned beef and we had to give them cans of peaches.

"These guys get spoiled fast," Phil complained. "Next they'll be attaching our pay checks to collect their fish bill."

For the last three days we had fresh beef. Buck wanted to shoot the gray bull but we talked him out of it. There were far better-looking cows to eat than that tough and ugly bull. "These things are going to be tough enough as it is," Phil said. "And the meat will probably taste of coconut, just like the water here."

We drove our cow down to the docks one afternoon, killing it and hung it on a hook. Phil butchered and dressed it out. It wasn't Grade A beef, but it was a change. We ate a great many pounds of it before we left the island. We ate steak for breakfast. Phil was right about the meat being stringy and tough, but wrong about the coconut taste. The meat had a wild taste, like venison. "Too bad we didn't have some eggs to go on top," Buck said.

For the nights, we had a Coleman lantern, but we were short of the round tube-wicks and fuel. We read or played cards or wrote letters home. Buck and Phil made necklaces of the "cat-eye" shells we gathered out on the reefs. They punched tiny holes in the shells and worked string into the holes, I never had the patience or the skill to do it.

Before we went to sleep we had our final swim, splashing in a puddle of starlight. The water was heavily phosphorescent. When someone dived, a shower of sparks went up. When we put our feet in, it stirred and sparkled like molten gold.

It was noisy down near the channel at night. The monkeys and the night birds cut loose in the jungle just across the channel. If they weren't noisy enough, we fired a few rounds in the air to stir them up. They were good, lively company. Sometimes we made night patrols up to the river to shoot at crocodiles. We never saw Snouts on the night patrol. "Strictly a day man," George said. We had considerable sport firing at crocodiles or at logs that looked like crocodiles, in the moonlight. We went to bed early to make our fuel for the lantern last.

In the morning we started out again. Our best days were spent diving from dugouts out along the reef. The cat-eyes we took out there were beautiful. There were octopuses and mantas, and the dorsal of a shark was not uncommon. We never had any battles with octopuses or sharks, but we did do a lot of firing at shark fins.

The Marines had their own method of fishing. They dropped explosives, TNT or composition C, on a long fuze down into the water. A great number of fish would be stunned by the concussion and come floating up. We did it once, but it seemed senseless killing. We had explosives, but we didn't use them, except the night we put on a fireworks display for the monkeys across the channel.

We lost track of the days. When the Higgins boat came out to get us, we couldn't believe that our time was gone. The scout sergeant who relieved us said: "How is it here, you guys?"

Phil said: "Awful. Drop off your provision and go back. We'll take your place."

But we couldn't arrange it. We had orders to go back and join our battalion. Buck had a better reason for getting in than we did. The rumor was that the ship taking the "old men" to the States was due in within a day or two.

"If they'd let me stay out here for the rest of the war," Buck said, "I'd almost pass up the boat ride back to the States."

The sergeant who relieved us said: "When you start talking like that, you *should* go home. You're island-happy."

In a way I know how Buck felt. It was wonderful to go back to the States, but it made men anxious, too. Some of them had been out almost three years. The Pacific almost was their home.

I've thought in the years that have passed that I would like to revisit our outpost. But it would be different. The plantation would be a booming business again. The cows would be back in their pens, and there wouldn't be a trace of the tent.

We came back to the rest base at Pavuvu ten days after we went out on outpost. The harbor was very busy. A transport was unloading more replacements. Another transport was standing by to take on old men who would be going home. A Dutch freighter was unloading new equipment and ammunition. The war wasn't over.

The company streets were so full and noisy with new men that Buck cringed at the sound of it. But then he said: "Well, heck, the kids' noise is normal. I'm getting Asiatic."

We found our tent just as we had left. Bob and Milt were all packed and ready to move on to the boat. Milt stood at the door of the tent and drew one long leg back like Bugs Bunny getting ready to take off. "Just sound that horn," Milt said. "And away I go like a swift rabbit."

The outfit was big and noisy again, and they were already running squad and platoon exercises in the grove. There was a rumor that there would be a battalion maneuver across Macquitti Bay. The dream, the wake, and the rest were over, and the Division was getting ready to go up again. I tried not to think about how it would be afterward.

8

RUMOR AND THE MAD GHOUL

The Mad Ghoul walked by night among the men of the First Marine Division, when the days of rest from Peleliu were blending into the days of preparation for the next campaign. There was never a clear break between the days. Gradually, the realization came that we were going up again; and in such times, strange things happen. The Ghoul, the dark knife-man who terrorized fifteen thousand armed Marines, was born out of the terror of men who had already seen awful things and who would see even more of them. If the Ghoul was born in fear, he grew on rumor. For Marines in the Pacific, there were few newspapers or radios to inform them of what went on in the world. Because they had no news, they created their own. Men made rumors and spread them; and other men believed them.

Rumors were white and black, good and bad. When the outfit first came off the line, the rumors were always hopelessly good. The Division, rumor had it, was through with fighting. We were going back to Australia or Hawaii, or even the States. Somebody had seen the shipping orders. . . . But we didn't go.

The Division settled into training for the next "push." The rumors changed from white to black. We were going into the worst campaign in the history of war. "They will stack the dead up on the beaches like pine board." . . . "I tell you this is *dinkum*: right now they're building scaling ladders. The attack will go right up the face of a cliff and into shore batteries." . . . "Mate, I want to give you the real scoop. This is no snow job. We unloaded bags of quicklime. You know what that means? They plow us into trenches with dozers and sprinkle lime. Too many dead to even bury." Men believed these rumors, too. I believed them. In such times it wasn't hard to believe in the Mad Ghoul.

The Mad Ghoul struck suddenly one night. We were out on outpost, and when we came back the Mad Ghoul scare was in full force. We didn't believe it at first, perhaps because the sun and the wind and the sea had washed all the fear and tension out of our minds. Buck left shortly afterwards for home, and never did believe it. But, later, the rest of us believed it. Reports varied, but the essential details of the Ghoul's first strike were these:

A rifleman woke one night—stirred, he claimed, by a prickly sense of danger, and aware that there was some sound strange to the tent and the company street outside. He lay on his back. The moonlight was strong, and all the tent-top was silvered with it and the company street seemed to lie under bright snow. He was an old man, who had lain through danger on the line, and he did not stir at first, but breathed quietly and listened.

Something whirred above his mosquito netting; there was the sound of tearing cloth; and a bright, shiny blade cut through the net above his eyes. The blade was drawn the length of the net, and when the netting parted the rifleman looked into the face of the Mad Ghoul. The Ghoul was dark—on this everyone agreed, then and later—big-jawed, blue-jowled and thick-lipped. His hands were heavy and furred on the back with black hair. The knife was long and unusually shiny. The rifleman screamed and upset the cot, rolling away from the Ghoul and spilling himself onto the packed earth of the tent floor.

One of the men in the tent tried to help his mate out of the tangle of net and cot. "Easy does it," the tent mate said. "You had a nightmare. Easy, boy."

"Nightmare, he says! Some guy was leaning over me with a big knife—a big, dark-faced guy, he was. And he seemed to be wearing fur gloves." The rifleman shuddered. Others in the tent woke. Some of the men in surrounding tents woke and called out questions and taunts. The rifleman insisted he had seen a dark man with a knife. Out of the darkness came taunts. "What's the matter with you guys in A Company? You can't even be quiet in a rest area."

The men in the tent tried to hush their mate. They were embarrassed. Everybody had nightmares, but the rifleman insisted on believing in his, even after he had been awakened. And the rifleman refused to go back to sleep. They put a pot of coffee on to boil over an open fire at the back of the tent. Men in the other tent protested against the light of the fire. Over and over, the rifleman said: "You guys know me. I don't spook so easy. I *seen* a dark guy with a knife. He almost stuck me with it." Finally he thought to examine the netting. It had been cut down its length by something very sharp. . . .

The word was passed from tent to tent. "Hey, his net was really cut! How do you figure that?" There was less kidding from the other tents. Two machine-gunners got dressed and came over to see for themselves. "I wouldn't trust one of you rifle guys to know a dark man from a dark coconut stump," one machine-gunner said. But once he had seen the net he had to admit: "This really was cut!"

So the Ghoul was born.

There was some talk of the knifeman in that particular battalion. But the talk died down and was lost amidst many other worse rumors. Three nights later, in another regiment, a company mortar man woke when something passed lightly across his throat. He looked directly into the Ghoul's eyes, and he described them: "Like a great big snake, they were."

The Ghoul had slashed away the net and he was running his knife, with tender care, across the throat of the mortar man. The man lay in terror for a moment, pinned to his cot by the Ghoul's eyes. Then he made a grab for the thick, hairy wrists. The Ghoul dropped his knife and clamped the mortar man's wrist in a terrible grip. When the man screamed, the Ghoul snatched up his knife and ran out of the tent.

Not so much doubting followed this "nightmare." A

company clerk at the end of the street had spotted a man running in the shadows. He saw the man hop over a tent rope and disappear into a thicket of scrub and fern. The mortar man—himself a strong man—had a sprained wrist. There was no mark on his neck. The touch of the Ghoul was skilled and delicate. That made the men more frightened. Few of the Marines were knifemen. They hated and despised men who used them. As they examined the man's wrist and slashed net, the company clerk came up with his story: "A big guy who moved like an animal—he went right by my tent." Everybody looked at the mortar man's wrist and slashed net.

The Ghoul was confirmed. Somebody else besides a sleeping man had seen the Ghoul. It couldn't be just a dream.

Everybody in the tents around the mortar man woke up and began to discuss the weird event. One man remembered the strange story he had heard from his buddy in another regiment about the first strike. He repeated as much of the story as he could remember. "I don't remember if my buddy over in A Company said the guy got cut up or not. I think he was. You were lucky."

Somebody else in the crowd said: "It must be some crazy man."

"Yeah. Some mad ghoul."

The Ghoul was christened.

Once he had a name, the story went all over the First Division. At the Division movie, men from the different regiments gathered in small groups to talk about the Mad Ghoul. In the middle of the picture some joker screamed horribly and yelled: "The Mad Ghoul strikes again!" A nervous neighbor turned and knocked the joker over one of the coconut-log benches. For some, the Ghoul was no longer a joking matter. Men who had gone through great danger on the line were terrified. A big, thick-armed rifleman complained: "I know what the Jap is up to. He's trying to kill you. But this nut—who knows about a crazy man, or whatever he is?"

The Ghoul struck again, five times in one night, in

different regiments and battalions. Details differed, but there was agreement on the big, dark man with the knife. At least three of the five strikes had to be jokes, perpetrated by men with strange senses of humor. The Ghoul had imitators, but there was no question about his existence. Everybody believed.

While the officers devised ways to explain away the Ghoul's existence, the men began to devise ways to explain him. I remember the discussion in our tent.

Chris said: "I can't understand it. Why would he be doing it? What's he want?"

George said: "I think he's some guy who has cracked up in an odd way. I mean he's psycho, but nobody has noticed it. Maybe in the day he's all right. He must be. He has to live with other guys. But then at night he goes off his head."

Tony, a new man, grunted: "He could be anybody—the guy in the next bunk."

Everybody looked at everybody else.

"You're kind of dark," someone told Tony.

"I'm dark," Tony agreed. "But I'm not tall. And besides I haven't been in combat and I haven't had the chance to go psycho like the rest of you."

Buster, a radioman, said: "There's one thing I notice. He hits on moonlight nights. There's a connection there. Course, these nuts always run wild when the moon is full. Watta you think, Dave?" he asked me.

I had been sitting on my cot trying to remember something I had been reading that was similar to the Mad Ghoul situation. Then I remembered, when Buster asked me the question. "Buster, look in that bookcase there. There's a book, *Days of Our Years* by Van Paassen. Get it for me."

Buster got the book and I began to read them a section from it. In it, Van Paassen wrote that a great, dark dog had nearly attacked him in a small town. This happened many nights, and finally the priest had been called in. The priest said that there was a girl in the village whose spirit was troubled. The evil came out of her in the form of a great, ugly dog. The priest then got rid of the spirit. I read them the whole section, while the fire flickered on the tent top.

"You don't believe it, do you?" Buster asked.

"I don't know," I said. "It's something to think about. There's plenty of troubled spirits in this Division."

"Plenty of evil ones, too," Buster said.

"There's one thing you might think about," I told them. "If this Ghoul is a member of the Division—and he must be—he lives in a tent with a lot of other guys. Now, to prowl he has to leave this tent in body. Think of it! He has to slip out, raise a howl, and get back in without being seen by six or seven other guys. This, when everybody in the Division is talking and thinking about the Mad Ghoul. Now, how could he do it?"

"You mean you don't think he leaves the tent?"

"*Something* leaves the tent," I said. "But whether it is the body of some Marine in the First Division, I don't know."

"Ghost stories," George said.

Chris said: "I wish you'd never mentioned your idea, Dave. I feel scareder now than I did before."

Buster said: "I say when the moon goes, the Ghoul goes. At least until the next full one. I believe in nuts. Some of my best friends are crazy. I don't believe in spirits—not the kind that carry knives and cut nets."

"We'll see," George said. "Dave has a point, though."

The moon disappeared, but the Ghoul did not. He hit again, in the darkness. This time, so the report went, twenty Marines from the Fifth Regiment chased him into the First Regiment area. It seemed certain that the twenty men had chased someone or something. A Marine from the Fifth said: "That proves it. The Ghoul is from the First."

"Proves nothing," a man from the First argued. "The last place he'd run is back to his tent. He's supposed to be crazy, not stupid. He probably ran into our area, circled around and went back into the Fifth—home sweet home for Ghouls. It's like I always figured. You guys in the Fifth read too many blood-and-thunder books. Keep your nuts over in your own area, willya, and don't chase 'em into ours."

Up to this point, there had been no official recognition of the Ghoul—at least in writing. An officer—somebody said it was the regimental recreation officer, who had quite a reputation for being a wit back in his home-town newspaper—wrote a paper in which he denied that such a thing, or things, person, or persons, existed. The title of the paper, which was supposed to be funny, was *There Is No Ghoul*.

Phil read the notice and told me: "Just as I thought. The Ghoul is an officer. They know who he is. They probably caught him coming back into officers' country one night. He may be over in the psycho ward at Banika, right now. So these clown officers try to make a joke out of it to hush it up."

That afternoon I heard the same story from a weapons man in the Seventh Regiment. "It's an officer all right. The Ghoul was an officer who wanted to get even with enlisted men. And he came from the Fifth Marines."

I couldn't understand why an officer wanted to get even with enlisted men, although I could believe that there were men who wouldn't mind carving up an officer or two. I found the information that he came from the Fifth Regiment very interesting. I could believe he came from anywhere but the First Marines. We didn't have such types, officers or enlisted men.

In the evening I was talking to a machine-gunner from the Fifth Marines and before I could give him my news he gave me his: "The Ghoul turned out to be an officer, all right. A buddy of mine over in the Seventh was in this guy's platoon. Seems some Marine enlisted man stole this guy's girl back in the States. They tell me it took three guys to hold him down in the Higgins boat. They always said he was big and strong, that Ghoul."

"Did you say he came from the Seventh?"

"Sure. Where else?"

"The guys in the Seventh say he came from the Fifth."

"That figures. They're covering up and tryna put the blame on us." He stabbed one thick thumb into my chest. "Look, Dave old buddy-buddy, the officers in the Fifth might be chicken and miserable. I ain't even sayin' we never had one duck up on the line. But they ain't crazy. We get the best that comes into this Division. Everybody knows the Fifth is the show outfit in this lash-up."

A hulking mortar man lumbered over and stood in front of the machine-gunner. "They're the show outfit, all right. Just like the First is the fighting outfit. All you jerks are, are a bunch of showboat guys." I walked away before the battle started.

At first the Ghoul was a half-serious joke. He hadn't killed anyone and hadn't even nicked anyone with his wicked blade. Then that changed. The story came around that he had slashed a Marine in the leg. It seemed certain that a Marine had been slashed. A corpsman from A Company told me: "I seen it. Good-sized nick all right. Five or six stitches at least. That part of it is fair *dinkum*. I wouldn't kid you a pound."

"How did it happen?" I asked.

"Guy is sleeping—light, of course, like everyone else these nights. Seems he hears the old rip and the Ghoul is coming down on him with the knife. Seems the guy throws his left leg up to protect his throat, and he claims he kicked the Ghoul a good one, but I doubt it. Anyway, he got a real slice taken out of his left leg."

In our Second Battalion, First, officer opinion divided. The commander of G Company put guards at either end of the company street. F Company organized voluntary guards. E Company, always very interested in volley ball and usually tired at night, ignored the whole thing. Headquarters Company drew up an official guard roster, but so many got excused from duty, for one reason or another, they couldn't fill their posts.

Long night walks and visits to other outfits began to drop off. Guards walked post with unloaded rifles, but with fixed bayonets. Some men carried their own personal pistols or knives in their pockets. It was about that time that I often went over to the First battalion to play bridge with friends in A Company and C Company. Chris told me: "I'd make new friends if I was you, Dave. One of these nights you're gonna get hit." If Chris hadn't mentioned it, I might have stopped my visits. Since he had, I had to continue them to show them I wasn't "chicken." It almost cost me my life.

We played late one night and the game drove all thoughts of the Ghoul from our minds. I was the only visitor from another battalion. Around midnight, a terrible scream came from a tent in B Company. Bart, a big squad leader from A Company, threw down his cards and yelled: "That's the Ghoul. That's our boy, Come on!" We all ran out onto the company street.

It wasn't the Ghoul. It was a rifleman having a nightmare about the Ghoul. That reminded me of the time and the Ghoul, I decided to go back to my battalion. Bart said. "There's a guard on our street, a new kid and real nervous. You'd better let me walk you back to the battalion boundary."

I was willing to have big Bart as company and we walked the length of C Company street and swung across B Company to the A Company tents. We had reached only the first tent row when a voice stopped us: "Halt!" It was a scared voice.

We stopped and jumped into the shadow of a coconut palm. There was no moon but the light from a distant campfire reflected on a leveled bayonet. It seemed to be wavering or trembling, but that might have been the light. The voice wavered: "What's the password?"

"I don't know," Bart admitted. "I didn't even know there was one. It's me, though: Bart. Don't shoot or do anything foolish."

"Move into the light with your hands high and clear," the voice commanded. It was steadier, after Bart had spoken. We scrambled into what light there was. Bart was as big as the Ghoul, but he was very blond. The guard said: "You near scared me to death, Bart. What you prowling around for?"

"Just checking to see if the guard was alert," Bart said. "It gives me a snug feeling to know that a brave fellow like you is alert and ready. Good work." Bart turned to me: "You're on your own, now. Think you can make your own outfit?"

I didn't answer him. I went across a softball field that made a no man's land between the First and Second Battalions. I was headed for the fire, which I knew would be in the tent of the company property sergeant. He belonged to our book club. About fifteen yards from his tent I stopped and yelled: "Hey, Joe! Joe! It's Dave." The fire was suddenly covered and there was darkness and silence and finally Joe yelled: "Walk into the light slowly. No foolishness now. Slowly." I walked slowly.

I stayed at Joe's tent for three cups of coffee. It wasn't good coffee but I didn't want to start for my tent alone. Nobody seemed to be walking my way that night.

Finally Joe said: "I think you should be on your way. Some of these kids are trigger-happy. You could get shot or stuck in the stomach with a bayonet."

"Or the Ghoul himself might grab you," a quartermaster sergeant said. "Last I heard he was waiting behind coconut trees. Just pulls the victim right in." He drew his finger across his throat and made a terrifying noise.

"Shut up," I told him. "I don't need that noise."

Joe walked over to the edge of the tent, but he was careful not to go outside the half moon of light thrown by the campfire.

"He's out there," Joe said in a low voice. "Sure as shootin' he's out there—prowling, waiting."

I didn't know whether Joe was scared or just kidding. Perhaps he was both. "Anybody walking my way?" I asked. My only hope was the quartermaster sergeant.

"I'm staying over here," the sergeant said. "I wouldn't walk two steps from this tent."

"I've got to get back."

Joe shook his head. "It's your funeral, boy. You're carrying a small piece, I suppose?"

I said, "I never carry a weapon off the lines."

"Wanta borrow mine?"

I shook my head. I was afraid if anything happened I

would panic and shoot some innocent guard. I took a deep
breath and stepped out into the darkness. Behind me, I
heard Joe and the sergeant sigh. It was a mournful sound.

I passed a row of dark, empty property tents and then
there was a gap, all dark, and then the company office
tent, and behind it the G Company street. I had to walk
across G, F, E, and Headquarters Companies to reach my
tent. At the foot of the G Company street was a line of
wash racks, and behind them the battalion shower, housed
in a thin wooden frame covered with white cloth. It was a
weird-looking thing in the dark. I knew it was the shower,
but when I reached it I debated whether or not to walk
around it and through an empty, coconut-littered gully, or
to go between the shower and the company street. I
decided to stick to civilization. There were men asleep in
the dark tents, I assured myself.

I never saw the guard. He must have been crouching
in the shadows of the company office tent. He must have
watched me sneaking along in the shadows and debating
whether to go around the shower or across the company
street by the wash racks. When I turned between the
wash racks, he thought I was the Ghoul swinging in to hit
someone in the tents. He landed on my back and his
weight bent me over the wash racks. I felt his bayonet in
the soft part of the back of my neck. I didn't struggle. I
didn't make any more sound than a grunt and a gurgle.
That saved me. Once he was on me and I didn't struggle,
the guard didn't know what to do next. He relaxed and
when he took his weight off my back, I slipped out from
under him and began to run. I think he yelled "Halt!" two
or three times, but I didn't hear him clearly as I ran. I
knew that he had an unloaded weapon, but running was
still stupid. Nevertheless, I ran—all the way back to my
tent.

I popped in under my mosquito net and lay there,
trying to quiet my heavy breathing. Fortunately, we had a
heavy snorer in the tent. Soon there was a stirring in the
whole battalion. Chris woke and talked to George who
talked to Jim. Jim came over, reached under my net and

shook me. "Hey, Dave," he said, "they just sighted the Ghoul over in G Company. He almost killed a guard. We're going over, wanna come?"

"No," I said. "I'm not interested. Besides I'm tired. I been running."

The Ghoul did not last much longer. According to reports, there were guards on every company street, and the military police made patrols all through the night. The Ghoul was sighted a few times, but always from a distance, and he was always running—perhaps from a guard. The report was that his hands almost touched the ground when he ran, and that he loped like an animal. Everyone knew that it was only a matter of time before they got him. Even a Ghoul couldn't beat the First Marine Division permanently.

Two or three dark men were turned into the military police by their "friends." They were questioned, but they turned out not to be the Ghoul, just strange men with strange friends. One man who wandered alone in the hills by night was picked up, but he was not the Ghoul, either. They sent him over to the hospital for an insomnia cure. After he had gone, the Ghoul was sighted running between the Fifth and First Marines.

The end came. The details seem reasonable enough to believe:

A guard sighted the Ghoul entering a tent over in Division Headquarters. The guard challenged, and the Ghoul began to run. He ran into a deep mangrove swamp. Military police ringed the swamp and word was sent to two armed military police in a radio jeep on the road beyond the swamp. The jeep patrol swung off the road and waited.

A big, dark man, wet and plastered with mud and panting as an animal would, broke out of the swamp and onto the road. A military policeman raised his .45 and commanded the dark man to halt. Instead, he turned and charged the armed military policeman. The military policeman shot him three times, close up, with a .45.

The Ghoul was dead.

*   *   *

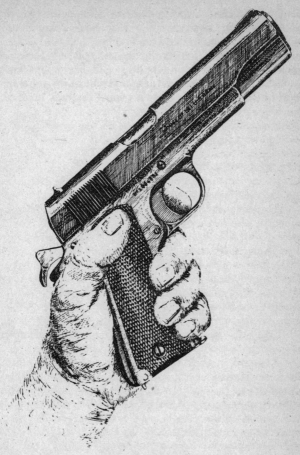

Colt .45 M1911 A1

There was no proof that such a creature as the Ghoul ever existed. But I believed in him at the time, and so did most of the Marines. Loneliness and a life in which rumor served as a morning newspaper could have created the Ghoul, spread his fame, and killed him. No one will ever really know.

That was how it was in the rest area, before we went up to another campaign. We read books, we went to movies, we played softball and volley ball and went to church; we wrote letters home and played cards and argued about religion and politics and lied about home. But in that time one character stands out in my memory— the Mad Ghoul. He was the dark spirit that was in all of us then.

9

BACK TO THE WAR

We were going "up" again. The next campaign came on like winter in the north, sending out signs of its coming. Instead of birds flying south in the night sky, ships appeared in the pink of evening out on Macquitti Bay and stood in toward our docks, bringing new men and guns for the next "push." Instead of a cold wind, winding in from distant snow fields, there was the chilling order from above: "End, forthwith, close-order drill, battalion inspections and regimental reviews. Begin, forthwith, squad, platoon and company exercises." Our days in rest and garrison were over. We were once more a combat outfit.

"We're going up," the rumors began. The whisper was everywhere.

"Where to?"

"North—where else? Maybe Formosa, the Bonin Islands, the China mainland—somewhere north." Men whispered of islands of which they had never heard three months before.

"Wherever it is we're going, it will be rough. I mean *rough*. They're building scaling ladders, more coffins, more crosses."

I began to sleep badly. Some nights I scarcely slept at all. I wasn't the only one. Late at night, when the tent flaps were turned up and I could look through into the other company areas, I saw a scattering of orange dots which marked men alone with their cigarettes and their thoughts and fears. They sat on the edges of their bunks and smoked through the night. Still no one would admit, aloud, that he was nervous in the night. Then he might become suspect by the others, and no one wanted to be cut off from the rest. This was the time when a man needed all the friends he had. This was the time when men sometimes told tales of their own bravery to remind themselves and their comrades that they were all good men.

When someone stirred in a tent and lit a cigarette, someone else would wake and a conversation would begin, but it would be careful and guarded.

"That you, Jack?"

"It's me. Just having a smoke. Nothing wrong."

"What's the matter?"

"Nothing. I told you nothing is wrong. Not a thing. It's the heat. And this jungle rot is itching me to death. I got myself scratched to pieces."

"Think the next one is going to be bad as they say, Jack?"

"They're all bad, buddy. Go to sleep."

We started training, but I did no more than go through the motions. Remembering the hopeless confusion of the last days on the line at Peleliu, I had no more faith in training. When the guns began to bang, everything would be a mess, anyway. Why make plans and play cowboys and Indians in the coconut grove? That was for new men. Old men knew better. The Guadalcanal men had been the same before Peleliu: John had refused to go on training exercises. Maybe he knew what was coming—a bullet through the head from a scared guard back in the Command Post.

A good line-company officer was named Battalion Three—in charge of plans and training for our Second Battalion. The Battalion Three called me in and asked: "How'd you like to be the operations sergeant for this battalion—my assistant?"

"What do I have to do?"

"Help me make up training schedules and plans."

"All right," I agreed. "I'd rather make them up than have to go on them."

While the rest of the troops went on exercises and fired out at the rifle range, the Battalion Three and I sat in a tent and made out schedules. A promotion came through and I was made corporal. This was fine. It meant that I no longer had to do mess duty or guard duty.

That Battalion Three and I had many long hours to talk, and he was the one who finally cured me of my nerves. He had been in many campaigns, and he liked to tell "sea stories." He got me telling stories of what happened on Peleliu; and somehow, in the telling, the campaign didn't seem so bad. I began to sleep nights again. It is said that men who have really seen combat refuse to talk about it. This never seemed true in the First Marines. The men talked among themselves about combat. There wasn't anything else very exciting to talk about. In the Pacific, telling "sea stories" helped to pass the time and relieve old pressures. I listened to thousands of them. I told them.

In January our regiment rode down through the Coral Sea on LCI's, bound for maneuvers on Guadalcanal. There, for the first time, I heard the name of the island we were going to invade—Okinawa.

A Battalion Command Post had been set up under towering ferns and behind the wide, paddle-shaped leaves of banana trees. It was just in from the edge of the jungle, but out of the worst of a driving rain which fell all during the morning exercises. The officer in charge of the battalion Intelligence section was sitting in the Command Post, huddled down in his poncho and shaking with an attack of malaria. Some of the headquarters men were clowning around, pulling on vines that were interlaced overhead up in the high branches of the jungle trees. Each time they yanked on the vines a shower of water fell on the men who were sitting on the floor of the jungle.

The Intelligence officer sat there in soaking misery, and finally he said: "Those clowns wouldn't be so frisky if they knew where we were going!"

"Where's that, Lieutenant?" I asked.

"Okinawa, in the Ryukyus."

I said nothing to that. It was the first time I had ever heard of the place. There was always the chance that it would be where I would leave my remains forever. I wanted to know more about Okinawa. That afternoon I went down to a Red Cross library and looked it up on a map.

It would be a rough campaign. The Japanese would have to defend an island that close to home with all they had left.

We finished maneuvers and returned to Pavuvu, and, although the rumors had now settled on Okinawa as the target, there was still no official notification for the troops. Combat Marines were always the last to learn about the next campaign. Usually some rifleman, who would be taking the most risk and therefore be least likely to give away the secret, learned of the target island from a clerk in a rear depot. We were supposed to begin training for fighting through streets, but Pavuvu had nothing but company streets between the tent rows. The men made a great joke out of the "street fighting." It started a rumor that Tokyo was the target.

We began a long course of inoculations. For some Marines this was torture; they feared the needle. I saw men dragged kicking and screaming down to the battalion sick bay to get their shots. Many Navy corpsmen were neither skilled nor gentle with the needle. For some it was a chance to pay back arrogant Marines who had bothered them. The medics told horror stories about giant shots given with huge needles in tender places. Some Marines half-believed them.

When a Marine bothered a medic there would be a snarl from the corpsman: "You won't act so big when we give you the old bicycle pump." The bicycle pump was the giant, legendary needle that navy medics used to scare noisy Marines.

When threatened with the "bicycle pump," the Marine would pretend to scorn such a story. "Stick that noise in your locker box, swabbie," the Marine would snarl.

"There ain't no bicycle pump. You thick-thumbed mechanics just make the little ones feel like big ones."

Still, under his show of bravado, the Marine was never sure. Anything was possible. One Marine told me: "Way I figure is, if it hurts we'll get it. Even if that big needle was full of tomato soup, the Marines would get it just to say they had the biggest shot ever given to man."

Attack transports began to gather out in the bay, and the men were put on shore parties to "combat-load" the boats. This was a serious job, because each ship had to be loaded so that the things that were needed first were the things that could be unloaded first. The work parties on the transports were very popular because they gave some Marines a fine opportunity to loot the transports.

Two stretcher-bearers, Murph and Chief, were the champion scroungers and looters of our battalion. When they came back to the tent at night, everyone in the company gathered around to see what they had taped to their legs, wound around their waists, stuck in their pockets, or even hidden in their mouths.

One old dock worker from New York said: "Boy, I never seen nothing like that Murph and Chief. After the war they could make a fortune down on the docks. I mean back home you can dress for it with a big, thick coat with lots of pockets. But here you work practically in a bathing suit. I mean it takes real ability."

The troops boarded the transports on March 1, 1945. On the day before that, I turned up with an impacted and badly infected wisdom tooth. I remember the look of horror on the face of the battalion dentist after he had peered into my mouth.

"Oh," he said. "Everything is packed. All I have is this old foot drill and I don't even think there's any Novocain. This would be a tough baby even if I had the equipment. Why don't you try one of the ships? Maybe they have a dental setup?"

My face was too swollen to talk clearly, but I managed to let the dentist know that I had tried other places first. He sighed and said: "Well, I'll have to cut through the gum and drill the thing into two or three sections to get it out. If you can take it, I can."

I remember the sweat dripping off his forehead as he worked, and how the corpsman pedaled the old foot drill. When he stuck his hands toward me with the extractor, the hair on his bare arms was slicked flat with sweat. He never tried to convince me "This won't hurt a bit." Nor did I try to pretend it wasn't hurting me. He puffed and sweated and I groaned and sweated and one corpsman couldn't stand watching and had to leave the tent. When the operation was finished, Murph and Chief had to take me back. Next morning when we loaded, they loaded me aboard on their stretcher. I missed taking a farewell look at Pavuvu, an island we were never to see again. I was in my bunk, too sick to see.

We had ship-to-shore rehearsals down off Tassafaronga, but I have no memory of them, except of being in a small boat in an enormous groundswell, seasick and with an infected jaw.

We sailed back to anchor off Banika, and we had shore leave in the transport area there. I was supposed to play in a battalion softball game and I lasted two innings before I had to lie down. I was too sick to move.

There were a lot of fights ashore in the transport area: the men were feeling ugly and tense. When we loaded again, it would be to go all the way to the target island.

Two weeks after we first boarded ship, we left the Russell Islands and there was no longer any secret about our destination. We were outbound for Okinawa by way of Ulithi.

My jaw healed but then I went down with malaria and, for two days and nights, I was in the transport sick bay, out of my head with fever and chills. I've had many attacks of malaria, and the sick dreams that go with them are always the same. I'm on an elevator that goes up and down with sickening shifts of direction and speed. *Up! Down!* There is a shuddering stop, and the whole elevator cage quivers and rocks. The motion makes me sick and I lie down on the floor of the elevator. The bottom drops out and I fall, down and down into sweaty, screaming consciousness.

Tony and George from the Intelligence section, and Murph and Chief, the scroungers and sometime stretcher-bearers, stayed up with me some nights, sponging my head and holding me down in the high, white bed. Murph was very skilled at forcing quinine into my mouth, even when I was out of my head. George tried it once and I bit him. Because Murph and Chief were scroungers they were invaluable friends. When I could hold it down, they brought in ice-cold orange juice and grapefruit juice, as well as other things.

When my two days on the malaria elevator were over, I was so hungry I couldn't get full. Thanks to Murph and Chief, I never ate better. Once Murph brought two dozen coffee rolls—a whole panful. He had secured a job helping the ship's baker. Chief was an assistant to the cook, and he had the key to the fruit locker. A "scrounger" in the Marines is a highly experienced artist and not a mere thief. The scrounger's idea is that everything is basically government property, and the government belongs to its citizens. As a citizen in good standing, the scrounger feels entitled to anything he can move, from an orange to a bulldozer or a cargo plane. The scrounger is not lazy. He will always volunteer for jobs, helping the baker or the cook or the medics. The scrounger who helps the baker, as Murph did, must know how to swap. As Murph said: "Man does not live by bread alone."

Murph swapped extra pastry for other commodities, such as orange juice and ice, sick-bay alcohol and ice cream, candy bars and the hair oil and lotion which Marines call "foo-foo" and love to smear on themselves. Murph's explanation of his activities on the ship went this way: "You got to have something to swap. If you got something to swap, then you're in business and you live fine. But you got to keep the store open all the time. Take this trip, now. I help the baker by taking away things before they get stale." Here Chief broke in on Murph: "You take them away before they even get cool, never mind stale."

"Like I said," Murph went on, "I get a bit of pastry now and again. I swap the pastry to the troops for hero gear" (battle souvenirs) "and I swap the hero gear to the swabbies for pogey bait" (candy).

Again Chief broke in: "And when the troops are short of hero gear we make our own. Some of my Rising Sun flags are better than the ones the Japs make. My Micronesian war clubs are better than you get on the islands. These natives don't have the equipment for production. I tried one sword," Chief admitted, "but it didn't come out so good."

"It was a good sword," Murph said. "We swapped it, didn't we?" To me, Murph explained: "Chief is a craftsman. He makes Indian relics back on the reservation."

With Murph and Chief to provide and to entertain, the ride to Ulithi passed quickly. On Murph's advice, I stayed in the sick bay until I was ordered out. Actually, someone threw my things out into the companionway and turned over my mattress. Murph and Chief helped me pick up my things. They weren't a bit disturbed. A scrounger has to accept insults, and they had done well in the sick bay.

While we gathered up my personal belongings, Chief said: "I pity the Marine who gets to ride on our stretcher. He'll have to lie right on Jap sabers or Mauser pistols or Arisaka rifles." He turned to Murph. "You 'member that guy who had to ride in on the Nambu machine gun?"

According to Chief, he and Murph always loaded their stretcher with battle souvenirs and then carried their wounded in on top of them. Officers, who used to commend Murph and Chief for struggling in with wounded under heavy fire, little realized that under the wounded were enough battle souvenirs to keep the store open for months. Just as

Arisaka Rifle

they didn't worry about insults, they didn't worry much about danger. They would go anywhere and endure any kind of fire if the pickings were good, and since they were fairly strong and had good endurance they brought in a lot of wounded Marines along with the hero gear.

Yes, Murph and Chief made the time pass quickly on the ride to Ulithi. I recuperated.

The troop holds smelled of sickness; the side decks were whipped with rain and slippery with spray from the roll of the ship; and over the front and rear decks swarmed the sea itself as the bucking, swaying transport clawed up waves and slammed down troughs. The last day and night we had been running through squalls, and the sea was still high-rolling when we came into the anchorage at Ulithi; and there, as far as we could look, until a dripping wet sky shut down on the far horizon, was the greatest gathering of ships in the history of the world.

There were transports, unending as common soldiers of the line. Patrol boats were like corporals; destroyers like sergeants; cruisers were lieutenants; carriers were colonels; and the battlewagons were generals. There was an army of ships arrayed in the anchorage at Ulithi. In such an army, the great Spanish Armada would have been run over and never sighted. There had never been as big a gathering before and there never has been anything as big since. Even the sickest and most bitter Marines came to the rail to look at the sea might of their country, and to feel, no matter how scared they were, some pride that the troops were the heart of the gatherings. The great ships were there to serve and protect the troops.

Chief looked at it all, shook his head in wonder, and asked a question that had occurred to all of us: "How can we lose?"

Murph said: "We can't lose. But you know something? This is the first time in this war I've really felt sure of it."

Everyone else agreed with Murph. After Ulithi there was never any question about our certain victory. The only

U.S.S. Franklin

question was *When?* For the next few days, as our transport moved around the anchorage, we hung at the rail, identifying the different ships. I had never seen a Landing Ship Dock (LSD) before. But there it was, with its high, blunt prow and its cranes. Ships could be put right inside it. I had never seen a new battlewagon or the big carriers. Our early carriers had been midgets. Even when we coasted by the dark and gaping holes blasted in the side of the carrier *Franklin*, we were sure that nothing could hurt us: we had too many ships. And even when the maps and photos of the beach and hills of Okinawa were brought aboard—when we could see the sea wall that had to be scaled, and the high swirls of ground beyond the beach— we still felt confident.

"This will be our last big one," the rumor said. "This will cave-in the Japs. We're throwing the whole bundle at 'em on this one."

It was D-day, H-hour plus 1, and I couldn't believe it. I was sitting midships on the transport, listening to the battle of Okinawa on the radio. The two assault regiments, Fifth and Seventh, had been ashore for an hour. Our First Regiment, because of the chewing it had taken on Peleliu, was landing in reserve. Buster had rigged up his radio with a high antenna and we were listening to the reports from ashore. The news was good. By bending close and listening through the static and the squawks, Buster caught enough to relay the news to the hundreds of men jammed around on the deck. "Resistance still light to moderate,"

Buster said to George. George cupped his hands and shouted to the crowd of riflemen: "Resistance still light to moderate."

A cheer went up, as though the home team had scored.

"How far in?" one old rifleman called. "I can see there's not much at the sea wall. What about the high ground?"

Buster bent to his set and listed some figures on a scrap of paper. "Look those up," he ordered Phil, who was keeping an informal situation map.

"Looks like about a thousand yards," Phil said. "It's over that first hump and about on line with Yontan airfield. I'd say they're moving up the high ground and not hitting much." George relayed Phil's estimate.

Another cheer went up from the crowd. It was like listening to a ball game on the barbershop radio. There were all kinds of military experts commenting on the situation.

"Get the Fifth Regiment," a rifleman urged Buster. "If there's any trouble there, the Fifth will stumble into it."

"I got 'em," Buster said. "Both Fifth and Seventh report light to moderate."

"If they say it's light, it's light," chortled one Marine. "They're glory-happy enough to make a fire-fight out of a misfire."

Buster suddenly stopped smiling and bent toward the set. There was a lot of squawking and popping, as somebody on the other end spoke directly into the mike from close up.

The crowd sensed trouble and surged forward toward the set. "What is it?" they called.

"Company patrol," Buster said. "Somebody got killed. Somebody hurt bad."

"Who?" George asked. "Who's hitting it?"

A rifleman put his hand over his face. "I knew it wouldn't last," he said. "Now it starts . . ."

"Hey," Buster said, "those aren't First Division call-signals. They must be from some doggie outfit. Yeah, maybe it's Army."

One of the Marines sighed with relief. It was a self-centered war.

"They ain't doggies," a Communication man argued. "They're Marines from some other division. Sounds like they're caught out on an open hill."

"It's the Sixth Marine Division," Buster said. "They must be up north somewhere. Listen to 'em holler. They must be gettin' it good."

"Give 'em some support," a Marine rifleman on the deck said. He clenched his fist and drove it forward. "Back 'em up," he said to some invisible listener. "Move in some fire power. Get 'em out of there!"

Around him old men winced and twisted as they imagined the fire pouring in on the ambushed patrol. Instinctively, even on the safe and protected deck, they hunched lower and spread out.

"They're pulling back." Buster said.

"Good. Get 'em off that hill."

There was a series of pops on the amplifier and then silence.

"How they doing?" somebody asked anxiously.

"I lost 'em," Buster said. "Either their man got hit or they're in defilade, or ducked into a cave."

"Switch back to the Fifth and Seventh," a rifleman said. "I like that ball game better."

An officer came along the deck. "How's it going?" he asked.

"Almost up to Sobe," Buster told him, "and no strain, no pain."

The officer nodded. "Get ready. We're going on in."

"What for?" a Marine rifleman asked him. "To carry the picnic baskets?"

"I'll take that duty," the officer said. "Let's go."

We climbed down nets into Higgins boats, an old-fashioned way of making an amphibious landing. As we went down, one rifleman said: "I just thought of what today is. It's April Fool's Day. That's why things are so funny ashore."

It was April 1, 1945.

"This may be one of the Japs' little April Fool jokes," a sergeant said. "They may be laying for us back in the hills."

I picked a comfortable seat in the bow of the Higgins boat and opened a book. "If the Japs are playing a joke, let's live it up while it lasts," I told the sergeant. "This is the kind of landings I like."

The coxswain backed the boat and swung it away toward shore. Men sprawled in it, looked completely relaxed. Several of the men had brought along books to read. Ashore, everything was silent except for engineers blowing a gap through the sea wall.

The coxswain looked at the Marines, reading and chatting in the boat. "This landing doesn't make any sense to me at all," he muttered. "Guys reading and sleeping as they go in."

"It makes sense to me, swab jockey," one of the Marines said. "This is the way civilized people should land on islands. I'm for this kind of landing. Are you with me, boys?"

"Aye," we all chorused. "We're for this kind of war."

In all the landing, there was only one violent scene. A kamikaze (Japanese suicide plane) screamed in under the guns of the picket ships, drove through wallowing transports like a ferret through a henyard, and exploded in a great orange flame against the side of a ship. We watched in horror as the plane screamed over our heads, lowering all the time until its wings were scarcely above the water. When it hit and disintegrated, one of the toughest riflemen in the boat blessed himself and said in awe: "How can any man do that with his life?" The kamikaze was a mindless and frightening thing, much worse for the Navy than for the Marines. Thousands of American sailors were going to die off Okinawa from the kamikazes, but we didn't realize that then.

I rode into the beach in Okinawa reading *The Glass Key*, a mystery—just like the landing. When I stepped out of the boat, not a shot was fired at us. It was the best kind of April Fool's joke I could imagine.

10

APRIL ON OKINAWA:
A PICNIC WITH GUNS

Above the landing beaches, the hills roll back in grassy folds to the plateau of Yontan; and from that plateau we could view the fleet lined up like toy boats, north to south in the China Sea. Our first position ashore was just below the ridge line, where we could still hear the demolitionists breaching the shoals and the sea wall. It was the only near sound of war, although far out in the haze there was an occasional spurt of "forties" and "twenties" from the picket ships riding the outer perimeter of the invasion fleet. I still could not believe I was witnessing a Marine D-day. Under a warm late-afternoon sun in a sky unsoiled with smoke, and on a grassy hill unscarred with bombs or shell fire, I stretched out and had a nap.

When I woke, the Battalion Three sat near me and I rolled over and said: "What are your orders, sir?"

He grinned and said: "Dig yourself in and set a good example for the new men." I dug a foxhole and made a back rest for my shoulders. The officers were holding a council, trying to decide what had happened to the war. The men were lying around in the sun. Just to the right of me a BAR man had made a beach umbrella by propping his poncho up on his weapon. "It's like Coney," a Brooklyn voice commented from behind me. "I mean it looks like the First Division landed on the beach at Coney Island by mistake."

In April the day heat died suddenly. Chill and damp came in with an onshore breeze, and the distant hills

40 mm's.

threw out long, purple shadows. As some of the old men
realized that night was coming on, the joking and horse-
play stopped and they began to dig.

An old squad leader said: "They're waiting for night to
come. Then they'll hit us good."

I didn't believe him, but I kept an eye on the dark
hills to the north. The Sixth Marine Division had turned
into those hills and, as night came, we could see the flash
of mortars and shellfire and the wink of tracers. A guard
was posted, but the only battle we fought that night was
with the April cold of Okinawa.

In the morning I woke stiff and drenched under a
soggy blanket. The heavy dew had sweated right through
the rubber poncho I had put over the blanket. I had put
some wood under my blanket to dry and I started a fire
and cooked breakfast for the Battalion Three, Captain Tex,

Murph and Chief. Murph was a welcome guest. Before he left the ship he had looted two tins of bacon and two dozen eggs. As he produced them from his pack he explained to the Battalion Three: "I had a feeling this would be a gentle landing. I didn't even break an egg."

"Murph," Captain Tex said, "until we have any casualities—and I hope that's never—I'm making you unofficial forager for this group." He waved inland. "Boy, this here island is your territory and I'm expectin' great things from you."

"Aye aye, Captain," Murph said. "I will carry away anything that can be moved."

We pushed directly across the island that morning. The Battalion Three sent me up with the lead company. We crossed a series of low hills and scouted through scrub pine and sandy ravines.

I was walking along with Ralph, the company scout, when rifle fire broke out just ahead. All the riflemen threw themselves down. Ralph stayed upright. "Don't let one rifle pin you all down," he yelled at them.

A rifleman said: "It only takes one to kill you." That was the rifleman's creed. For them, it made no difference whether they were killed by heavy artillery in a big battle, or by one lone sniper in a patrol action. "You're just as dead," the rifleman said. "This looks like a soft campaign and I want to live through it. You be brave."

Ralph and I ran forward to where the "point" (lead riflemen) had gone down into a stoop squat below a wall. The sergeant in the point waved toward a pine thicket on the side of the hill. "Jap came down through there and opened up on us," he told Ralph.

The platoon lieutenant moved up behind the wall with us. He waved out two flanking squads to work around the thicket on either side. They moved out but there was no sound of firing. As soon as they joined, they called for us to come through the thicket. "That Jap took off like a big bird," the leader of one of the squads said.

That was the only action in the battalion that day. We had orders to halt early and dig in for the night. There was another officers' conference as they tried to guess what the

Japanese were planning to do. Nobody ever expected the Japanese to quit without a fight: they never did. No Marine in the First Division ever doubted the courage of Japanese soldiers.

When the Battalion Three came back from the conference, he said: "Now, we got to be careful. If we keep running across the island at this rate, some of the men are going to fall into the Pacific on the other side." He shook his head. "Nobody, from the General on down, knows what to make of it. Already we've covered more ground that we did during the whole Peleliu push. And still no Japs."

"Maybe we got the Japs scared," said one new rifleman.

Everybody laughed. "The Japs just don't get scared," somebody told him. "You'll see."

On the third day we reached the Philippine Sea at the opposite side of the island. It was early afternoon when we patrolled into a town of plywood and cardboard houses which, though flimsy, were still standing despite the shelling. Below the town was a long slope of brown grass and far down at sea level, deep green rice paddies. Red tiles of a fishing village showed beyond the paddies and beyond the roofs of the village was the sea. It was a good sight and we squatted on the grass outside the village to look down on it. Some of the men scrounged through the flimsy houses.

We heard a single shot and then a burst of Tommy-gun fire. We all rolled over in the grass and stretched out and faced the sound of the firing. A lieutenant ran by and yelled at us: "Jap soldier just ducked into one of the houses." He waved us forward and we all crept up on the house. From about five feet out, we sprayed it with rifle fire until it almost disappeared in a puff of papier-mâché and cardboard. The walls caught fire and the whole house exploded. One big mortar man, who was charging it head down, drove right through the walls and was blown out the other side by the blast. He landed on his back beyond the house, singed and cursing, and somebody dumped a helmet full of dirty water over him. We did not find any trace of the Japanese soldier.

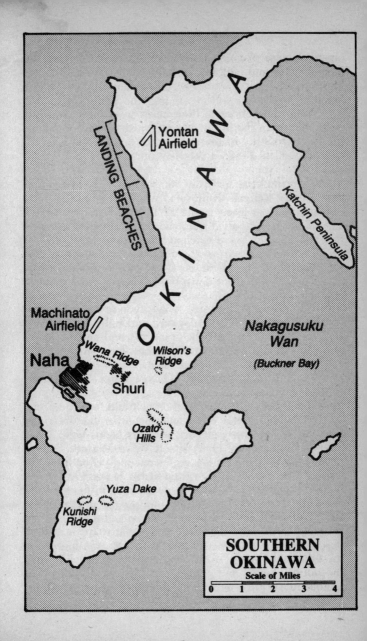

SOUTHERN OKINAWA

Scale of Miles

0 1 2 3 4

In any group there are sadists, men who delight in doing damage and inflicting pain. As soon as we had blown up the first house, a group began systematically to fire the other houses in the village. Before the lieutenant and I could stop them, most of the houses were afire, and the lovely village on the hill was leveled just because someone thought he saw a Japanese soldier run into one of them. I went forward and joined another company.

At nightfall the company had reached the sea and the base of the Katchin Peninsula, where the purple hills appeared to float loose in the Philippine Sea. We turned back inland and climbed from the paddies toward a crumbling coral ridge. As we reached the bottom of the ridge, a machine gun opened up on us. It was an American gun and it was fired directly at us. There was no mistake about either fact. We all went down behind a projecting spine of coral and began to yell.

The platoon leader said, "Davis, you're well known to the whole battalion. Crawl forward and tell them who we are." I crept out around the spine of coral and began to yell. They answered me with a second long burst.

"Stand up," the lieutenant said.

"Drop dead, Lieutenant," I advised him. "If you want to do this, come on out here."

I forced myself into a half-crouch and, with one eye on the shelter of the rocks and the other on the ridge above, I moved slowly forward with my hands high. I was yelling: "Don't shoot! Don't shoot! We're Marines!"

"Don't listen to him, boys," someone yelled from the ridge. "That's no Marine. Listen at his Jap accent."

The machine gun began to go again and I flung myself down flat. This time I could tell from the sound of it that it was aimed high over my head. I got up and dusted myself off. I had even recognized the voice that went on yelling from up on the darkened ridge: "All right, you lousy Jap! We know where you're at. You cain't fool us with such turrible English."

The voice belonged to Reb, machine-gunner from Georgia, who was an old friend of mine. Only the week before I had offered to give Reb English lessons, and he was paying me back for the insult.

The lieutenant had also recognized the voice and he bellowed with anger. "All right, Reb. The joke is over. We're coming in. You stop the nonsense."

When I came over the ridge, the first grinning face I saw was Reb's. "Why didn't y'all send someone forward who could speak English?" he asked. "Lucky for y'all the lieutenant is from Maryland. I kin half understan' him, when he speaks clearly."

"Lucky for me they had you on the gun," I said. "I got worried when I realized you were shooting into the air. I was sure you'd hit me."

For the lieutenant, the incident hadn't quite ended. He called me over, and in front of all the men said: "Davis, I know there was a lot of excitement out there, but at one point it almost sounded as if you told me to drop dead. I'm sure we all must have misheard you."

I looked as shocked as I could. I knew the lieutenant; I liked him, and I knew he was just re-establishing discipline.

"Lieutenant," I assured him, "there is no officer or enlisted man in this regiment or division for whom I wish a longer and more happy life than you, sir. I respect you, admire you, even love—"

I could see the lieutenant grinning in the darkness as he interrupted me. "All right, Davis," he broke in, "we don't need any speech. I was just checking."

The lieutenant did get through the campaign, and for that I was glad. We were very superstitious about wishing harm to anyone, and I worried about that lieutenant's health until the campaign was over and he was safe.

The next day we made a long patrol down the Katchin Peninsula, but nothing came out of it but blisters and sunburned necks. Wherever the Japanese were, they were not in the middle of the island. We came back inland and set up a bivouac area. There were rumors that the Sixth Marine Division was running into some Japanese in the

north and that the Army divisions were hitting heavy
resistance in the south. These rumors happened to be
true.

A new major came in as Battalion Three, and my old
boss went on to a new job in Regimental Headquarters. It
was a fair swap. The new Battalion Three was the best
Marine officer I ever served under. Some officers let the
enlisted men dig their foxholes or put up their shelters,
but the new major was so strong that he would have our
position finished before I could get the entrenching tool
off my pack. At the time, we were sleeping inside Okinawa
houses, but we had foxholes prepared outside for the night
air-raids. At first, when "Condition Red" was flashed, we
would run out of the house and sit in the shelters. After a
few nights, we ignored the raid unless they dropped
bombs close by or made a strafing run on our house.

In bivouac the talents of Murph and Chief were
important. They ranged out of the area for miles, raiding
gardens for onions and potatoes, looting houses of lacquerware dishes, tablecloths and fancy wall-panels with which
they lined their foxholes. Murph put a *tatami* (mat) floor in
his foxhole. In best Japanese tradition, no one was allowed
to enter unless he took his shoes off first. From somewhere Murph got clean sheets and he slept between
them. His greatest find, however, was an alarm clock. This
was much admired and men came from other outfits to see
it. Looking at it, one old office worker sighed and said, "I
never thought I'd be glad to see one of those gadgets
again. But it makes me homesick."

Murph quickly learned all the crops in the field and
he and Chief prepared their ration stew with a delicious
assortment of herbs and roots. Murph had contacts back
on the beach and he was always provided with the newest
and most select C-rations and ten-in-one rations. He found
a store of sweet potatoes and scallions and, in one raid, he
came in with ten eggs and two tough old roosters. We
boiled them.

The Chief and other Indian friends rounded up some
horses which they used for packing in the loot. In their
free time they had bareback riding contests. One Indian

named Andy used to come tearing and whooping down the road like a plains Indian raiding a wagon train. The greatest coup counted by Murph and Chief was a hog which they caught, butchered, and dressed. We had fresh pork for several feasts.

During that first month on Okinawa we camped out at government expense. We had no other problem except how to make ourselves as comfortable as we could, and we did just that. We slept on the best *tatami* mats, ate off the best lacquerware dishes and raided the fields and the farmyards for whatever crops or livestock were available. When we could get back into the rear areas we shared the hospitality of the Seabees (Naval Construction Battalions). Among the Marines the Seabees had a reputation for great ingenuity and unfailing hospitality, and they were like older brothers or fathers to the young Marine riflemen. Mruph particularly admired Seabees. Murph said: "Put a Seabee down alone in the desert and he'll find a way to start an ice-cream plant."

We had no movies on Okinawa because of the air raids, but the battalion had a radio. Each night we gathered in a field around the radio jeep and listened to the news from home. Favorite programs were the Japanese propaganda and morale broadcasts made by Tokyo Rose and Shanghai Betty. These two ladies came on the air every night. They were supposed to make the men homesick and ready to quit the lonely war in the Pacific, but actually their effect was opposite. They provided more entertainment than the U.S.O.

Both Rose and Betty had their own fan clubs among the Marines, but with our outfit Rose was more popular. She had a sense of humor. She played good records and she took special delight in dedicating them to the men in the First Marine Division.

Right after nightfall there would be a hundred cigarettes aglow in the field: all would be hushed and the radio would be turned up high. Suddenly, the purr would come: *"This is your sweetheart, Tokyo Rose. I'd like to dedicate the next number to the men of the First Marine Division."*

"Atta baby, Rose," some Marine encouraged her. "We're

going to dedicate this island to you, soon as we take it."

Talking softly and smoothly, Rose would say. *"This Number is* 'I Don't Stand a Ghost of a Chance' *and it's very appropriate for the men of the First, now on Okinawa. We know you're there, boys, and, believe me, you don't stand a ghost of a chance. It makes me sad to think how little chance you really stand. You'll all die there."*

"Aw, Rosie," some Marine would beg her. "Don't be morbid. Play the music and stop worrying."

And finally the music would come and the men would lean back on their elbows and drive smoke up into the darkness and wish they were back home, listening to a dance band.

Sometimes Rose closed the program with a salute or tribute to the Marines: *"Good night, men, wherever you are. I only wish there would be more of you alive tomorrow night. Aren't you tired of being the goats, while your smart friends are back in the States, dating your girls and eating steaks?"* She would then sigh, loudly and sadly. *"Well, good night."*

It was from the radio jeep that we heard the news of President Roosevelt's death. Nobody would believe it. They thought it was a propaganda trick. "President Roosevelt couldn't just die like that," one Marine said.

This was a tribute to the President's reputation for being enduring. He had been President for as long as some men could remember. Also, the Marines always found it difficult to believe that anyone was dying back home. Though a man might have seen five young friends killed in a single afternoon, he was shocked to read of the death of one elderly relative. When the news came that my grandfather, whom I loved greatly, had died, it took me two months before I believed it; and I never did truly believe it until I went home and walked down to the house he had lived in and saw that it was deserted. We expected the world back home to stay exactly as it was when we left it. For this reason, homecoming was always a shock.

After the announcement of the president's death, most of the men drifted away from the radio early. It seemed disloyal to listen to Tokyo Rose that night, and many of the men gave up the small entertainment they had as a token of mourning for the President. We went back and sat around and drank coffee and talked.

An old mine worker said: "Some of you don't remember back in the early '30's. But in my town we didn't have a bean for the pot till Roosevelt come in. Then he help us!"

"He was a great man," somebody said. "Like Churchill."

"No," the miner said. "More than Churchill. Churchill is jes' snowin' those limeys so when they win the war they come back to the same lousy thing—nothin'. But our guy woulda done somethin' for us. . . . I wish he din't die."

Murph, who was a Pole like the miner, said: "Well, Stash, you see a lot of young guys die around here. What about them?"

"What you expect?" Stash asked. "That's what we're here for."

11

FIRST ASSAULT ON THE
NAHA–SHURI LINE

The password that night was "Ali Baba." The Marines used passwords with an *l* sound in them because the Japanese pronounce it *r*. In the darkness, just inside the company perimeter, a sentry called: "Halt! Who goes there?"

Silence. And then a scrambling sound out in the darkness. Then silence again.

We felt for our weapons and turned in the direction of the challenge. Off to the west there was sky glow and the muted thud of heavy antiaircraft batteries—.90's. Into the light reflected from the sky crawled Captain Tex, tilting his .45 upward to get a clip seated and worming up the bank, using only his knees for purchase. There was a loud, metallic rip as the bolt went back on somebody's Tommy gun.

"Answer up or I'll blast you," the sentry yelled.

This challenge was higher-pitched and slightly quavery, the kind a man delivered when his scalp prickled and his eyes strained into silent darkness. "What's the password?" This was screamed.

Terror bred terror. From the darkness, a quaking Midwestern voice twanged: "I forgot it. I forgot the bloody, blankety-blank password."

Whoever was out there in the darkness was scared, but he was doing the next best thing to remembering the password—he was using bad language, the sign of a Ma-

140

90 mm AA

rine under tension. We could almost hear him wetting his lips for another try. Then he said: "I got a message from the colonel for Captain Tex. I mean Captain—Aw, I forget his name, too. You know the captain I mean. That crazy Texas guy in Headquarters Company."

There was a sigh of released tension in the holes all around us. I could feel Murph begin to shake with silent laughter. Captain Tex bellowed: "Don't let that man through until he gives the proper password and the name of the man who gets the message. There is no crazy Texan in this sector—or anywhere."

The sentry relaxed after he heard the captain's voice,

but he still sounded stern as he called: "All right, you out there. You got ten seconds to think of the password. Get it up or I'll begin to chop!"

There was a full minute of silence, and, finally, a weak and muffled voice, coming from a man who was well down in a hole or behind a wall: "Twenty thieves . . . Yeah, that's it—twenty thieves."

All through the darkness men began to laugh: "Twenty thieves," some rifleman chuckled. "How about that?"

Captain Tex's voice carried above the laughter. "Don't shoot him over twenty lousy thieves. Only a Marine could be that bad in arithmetic."

"Pass, friend," the sentry said. "And hear this, you knucklehead. The password is Ali Baba—with an *l* in it. And old Ali dealt with forty thieves—not twenty. The captain, who is right over there, may have other things to say to you."

The captain stood up. This was a good moment for him, because he was a constant needler and jokester. "Young man," he began, "you have made many mistakes tonight. You forgot the password. You forgot my name. You are bad in arithmetic and have no knowledge of literature, and you can't even tell a sane man from a crazy one. What state do you come from?"

"Minnesota, sir."

"An outpost of Northern ignorance," Captain Tex said. "Now, after all this, I'll bet you've forgotten the message."

We all laughed. It was our last good laugh on Okinawa.

The messenger hadn't forgotten the message. It was the one that brought an end to the camp-out and picnic on Okinawa. The message informed us that we had been ordered south to relieve the 27th Army Division on the Naha–Shuri line. There was no longer any mystery about where the Japanese were on Okinawa: they were defending the middle of the southern part of the island, in a line running from Naha Harbor, through Shuri, and on to the Philippine Sea near Yonabaru. Here they defended stubbornly, fanatically, desperately. Here was the Japanese 32nd Army, putting up a fight-to-the-death defense, from deep caves and vaults in the ridges. On the Naha–Shuri line, the Army had been catching it. Out on the picket line, the Navy ships had been catching it from the kamikazes. The Marines had been camping out at government expense—and that couldn't last.

Murph said, "Here's where we pay for all the C-rations we ate."

"You're right," Captain Tex said. "Let's get one more good night's sleep while we can. From now on it will be bad."

We rolled from the sway of the trucks, bobbed from the jolt of them, coughed from the fumes of them, and were stained khaki by the dust of them; but we minded only one thing—the sound of guns rolling downwind from the Naha–Shuri line. We were moving south to the line, within sight of the China Sea; but the sound of the sea was lost in a mightier roar that was like the roll of drums endlessly held. The artillery was plastering the Naha–Shuri line approach, from Machinato to Wilson's Ridge. When we rounded the corners of the coral bluffs we expected to see the battlefield, but we saw only more hills and a pall of smoke far ahead. The smoke might have been hanging over an industrial city, but we knew it wasn't. It marked the place where the Japanese had decided to fight and die.

Each time a man moves up to the line, he must nerve himself against the sound of war. We were out of practice and our nerves were not in shape for the slam of the guns. When the guns slammed, some men gritted their teeth; other clenched their fists or blinked or bobbed their heads or jumped. Some men settled into a steady trembling and ducked down below the steel sides of the truck, even though we were far out of range of enemy fire.

Moving up to the line in trucks did not have the dash and color we had known when we roared into a beach in the amphibious tractors. We were amphibious men. In the truck convoy there was none of that inspired momentum that comes when a long line of small boats wheels and drives in on a defended beach. We were commuting to work from the suburbs of the war, and the job ahead would be a dangerous, slogging grind, as dull as office routine. We thought we had escaped when our beach turned out to be soft and easy; we no longer had any enthusiasm for the campaign. They were placing us in double jeopardy; and we were like men hanged for a second time after the rope broke on a first try.

The road went between twin bluffs and we had arrived at an assembly area where trucks backed and circled in a dusty clearing. The command came: "Off-load. Assembled in a column-of-twos on the road."

For the rest of the way we would walk, or perhaps crawl forward. But we would go forward. Of that every man in the First Marines was certain. We never realized the possibility of going any other way. "We go forward or we hold what we got," one colonel told me. "That's all there is to it."

The troops strung out along the right-hand side of the road and moved ahead in a column-of-twos. At first there was lurching and straggling as the men settled in against the weight of their transport packs and the discomfort of weapons and a full unit of ammunition. There was no sound but the squeak of canteen holders in cartridge belts, the slap of helmet straps or the metallic rap of a rifle butt on a box of machine-gun ammunition. Some of the older men began to breathe heavily. A few of the newer men frisked around to right and left on the roadside and sometimes stopped to look at shell cases or abandoned equipment, but they soon settled into routine march and a silence settled on the files.

A tall mortarman carried the tube, balanced on one shoulder like a log; a second man carried the bipod; a third, squat and powerful grunted under the carrying straps as he lugged the heavy base plate. These were men from the heavy mortars. The men with the .60's swung along up ahead with the rifle companies. They didn't have as heavy loads but their ammunition was hand-carried.

Riflemen carried their weapons in every way except the way they are carried in a parade. Some had the rifles tucked under their arms, as though they were hunting upland birds. Some carried their weapons across their neck and shoulders and held onto both ends; other carried the piece over one shoulder and gripped the muzzle in one hand. The men with small carbines carried their pieces slung. BAR men shifted their long rifles from sling to shoulder to back; their assistants wore sagging belts of BAR magazines and carried an M–1 with a full "unit of fire" (ammunition allotment). Machine-gunners, mostly with light guns but a few with "heavies," toted their tripods and guns and metal boxes of ammunition and wore belted .45's. Radiomen packed their 300's and also carbines; bazooka men packed their tubes and shells; demolitionists carried bulging, dangerous packs. But the flame-thrower men carried the heaviest and worst burden of all. Most of them were heavy-shouldered men. Out in front of the column prowled Tommy-gunners. The line was not close enough to make a "point" necessary, but some men had been sent out anyway to scout the front and sides. Every man carried a weapon and every man walked—that was a Marine Infantry battalion.

Down the line came the word: "Doggies coming back. Doggies coming. Here comes the Twenty-seventh Division,

Before the men from the Twenty-seventh Division, Army, appeared, I saw the shoulders of the Marines straighten all along the file. Weapons which had almost been dragging on the ground were raised and carried smartly, and the side straggle of the column pinched in and they formed a neater column of twos. Eyes turned left as the Infantry column came down the other side of the road.

The men of the Twenty-seventh did not look at the Marines. They said nothing. One Marine made a crack but he was silenced by other Marines. The infantrymen were quiet, dirty and dispirited, turned into zombies by days and nights on the line. The Marines were thoughtful and quiet, knowing it was always possible for them to come out the same way—if they came out at all. The two outfits passed each other silently.

Near Machinato, our Second Battalion swung off the road and went down toward the sea to hold a reserve area behind the First and Third Battalions. The Battalion Three and a lieutenant and I went up to look over the lines and to pick out a spot for an Observation Post. We started into a destroyed village, moving down a street that was littered with splintered panels, torn mats, up-ended farm carts and smashed tiles. Near the end of the street was a high concrete wall. It had been breached many times with artillery fire. The major waved us down to a squat and we crept along the wall. We judged that we were either on the front line or just in back of it, but there were no troops there. The artillery fire overhead was steady.

"Wow!" the major said. He was peering around the corner of the wall. "Look at that!"

We crawled up behind the major and peeked over his head. I gasped and squirmed back. Beyond the edge of the wall, the ridge ended. There was a long roll into the valley below. Far across the valley, beyond low hills and one east-west escarpment, was Shuri itself. The castle and the Japanese barracks were clearly in view. There were flashes and spurts of smoke and debris all along the Shuri Ridge. "Look at the view," the major urged us. "This is our Observation Post."

"You could fall right out of this village," I told him.

"But what a view!"

As he spoke, the smoke that masked Shuri ridge was split by the flash of an exploding shell and the walls of the castle loomed. Off beyond a coastal flat near the China Sea, Naha—the largest city on the island—smoldered like a city dump. Between Naha and the escarpments in front of Shuri were rounded, grassy knobs. We studied the ground. We were getting a preview of the country in which we would fight our war for Okinawa. It was a frightening sight.

At nightfall we came back to our camping place—a concrete amphitheater formed by the entry to a huge burial vault. Even before I shredded explosive to make a quick fire for my coffee, and before I laid down my poncho for a ground cloth, a restless night had begun on the line. Flares popped overhead and the walls of the burial vault were frescoed with green shadows. Below in the message center we could hear the calls coming in from the line companies:

"Illumination in G Company."

"Get some flares up over F Company."

"First Platoon of E Company reports infiltration down by the sea wall."

The company mortars fired; the battalion mortars fired; the artillery fired; the naval guns put up flares. A bad night had begun.

The major and I sat with our backs against the vault and drank our coffee. Off near the sea wall a rifle fired once. A machine gun rattled in a long-winded burst. A BAR tapped away aimlessly. Listening to it, the major said: "I remember a story about a blind shoemaker who tapped away for years while he waited for his enemy to come back. He wasn't making shoes, just making noise while he waited. That's how that sounds."

"It sounds like a symphony tuning up," I told him. "We'll be taking a part in it soon enough."

"I suppose so," the major sighed. "Let's see if we can get some sleep now."

Full spring morning had come, and though there was no heat the sun had pulled the dampness out of the earth and the hillsides were warm to sit against. We sat and watched the company which was getting ready to attack through a gap in the ridge. On either side of the gap were high sand banks; behind it was a destroyed village; out ahead were Japanese machine gunners with everything laid in on the gap.

We were waiting to see what the company commander would do about the gap. That captain had the reputation of being a wild man. They called him "Gung Ho," "Old Blood and Guts," "Wahoo Willie" and other names to show he had more nerve than brains. He was the kind of Marine officer who did well enough as long as he never had to make a decision involving more than one choice. At that moment he was pacing up and down, just back of the gap, and he was angry.

The riflemen were plastered against the banks on either side. They were calling for mortar fire and artillery support, but nobody seemed to have any particular target in mind. The company commander didn't trust maps. When he wanted artillery support, he waved at a piece of ground and growled: "Plaster it!" He had two good decorations for bravery from other campaigns, but he couldn't read a map.

"What will the Wild One do?" I asked Ralph, the scout in that company.

"I don't know. He'd like to call for a bayonet charge. I mean if he could find somebody to stick the old cold steel into, that's what he'd do. But those Jap gunners are down in bunkers somewhere. Maybe he'll pull his pistol and go whooping through. I couldn't say."

I was wishing that the major were there to steady the company commander. The captain was pacing up and down, chewing his lip and looking wall-eyed at the gap. His platoon leader dropped back to confer with him—and we could hear them.

"We just can't get through," the platoon leader told the commander. The platoon leader was down on one knee and resting his weight on his carbine. He tried to reason with the commander. "We should wait for tanks," he advised.

The captain snorted. "Tanks! Man, we gotta get through that gap. I don't know about no tanks."

Ralph said of the platoon leader: "He's a good young officer. I hope Willie doesn't get 'im killed on this thing. Willie ain't waiting for no tanks. He thinks it's not playing the game to use tanks."

The other company scout came over and sat down beside us. His name was Sam, and back in the States he had been a genuine working cowboy. "We goin' through?" he asked Ralph.

"Not in one piece we're not."

We heard the captain say, "I know there's no cover on the other side. You got to ram through there and spread out fast when you hit the other side."

He glared at the gap. He hated it. He hated any hill,

river, mountain or draw that got in his way. He was a former football hero, and to him every piece of bad terrain was a tough line on the other team. He wanted to bust through it with his head and shoulder down.

The lieutenant was raising his voice, too. "There's no cover for fifty yards on the other side, Captain."

"Fifty yards!" the commander bellowed. He snorted. He was probably remembering how fast he had covered fifty yards in a football stadium. He paced up and down again, glancing over his shoulder as though he were getting ready to perform before a great crowd in the stadium.

Murph, who was watching the captain, said, "All he needs is a brass band and a few cheer-leaders."

"In his mind he hears a thousand cheers," I agreed. "He's about to do or die for old State."

"He'll die," Chief said flatly. Nobody argued that statement. The captain stopped pacing and called loudly, "I'm gonna show ya! I'm gonna drive through that hole there. I'm gonna drive through and find cover on the other side. And when I get through I want you to bring the boys through. Clear?"

"I don't think—" the lieutenant began.

"Think!" the captain yelled. "*Think?*"

"The worst possible word," Ralph said. "He hates that word. Now he'll go."

"A few machine guns holding up a whole company of Marines!" the captain said. "You got to take a few casualties in a war."

"He throws away men like they were going out of style," Ralph said. "He's going to go."

It was clear that the captain was going through the gap alone. He checked the crowd in the stands with his over-the-shoulder glance, rolled his shoulders and swung his arms, hopped a few times to loosen up his legs and pulled his pistol. He looked at his pistol, looked at the gap, and then holstered his pistol. Even he could see that it would do him no good, and it might slow him down.

The captain got down like a halfback, with his knuckles resting lightly on the blasted earth. He seemed to be listening for some phantom signal which would tell him when the ball had been snapped and he was to set off down field. It came. He drove forward—going low through the gap, weaving with his shoulders and head—faking as though he were driving through the secondary; straightening

Nambu

for more open field speed, and side-stepping with his knees going high. He was a big, beautifully balanced man, doing a most stupid thing.

The machine gun caught him as he side-stepped some imaginary tackler. It was a Nambu, which fired faster than a tackler could blink, and it spun the captain off balance, but he regained his feet and drove on. Then two guns went after him in tandem and he folded in the middle, stumbled and plunged forward headfirst, still churning with his legs for that extra yardage, right up until the time his nose plowed into the yellow dirt. Once he went down, he never even twitched. He had driven the last two yards stone-dead.

"Oh," Murph said. "Oh!"

The riflemen were stunned for a moment and then someone yelled and two men ran up the bank, and in a frenzy began to fire over the top. One man cursed in a very loud voice and began to run toward the gap, and others followed him. In one swirl the platoon went driving through. Only one man was hit, and he was hit lightly.

The captain had been very well liked by most of his men. As Murph and the Chief brought him back, the corpsman said, "I never seen a guy take more hits. He was a real horse."

The captain was the first man I saw killed on the Naha–Shuri line. He was one I could never forget. He died with great dash and derring-do. Few other men did that, even in the Marines.

12

BREAKTHROUGH AT SHURI

We fought for every one of those round knobs in front of Shuri ridge—fought up one side and down the other. The reverse slope fighting was the worst because there the Japs had dug in deeply and they had to be "shoe-horned" out or sealed into their bunkers by tank-infantry teams. "Tank chasing" (use of foot men to protect tanks) became one of the most dreaded chores of the riflemen. After I had chased once with a rifle squad, I understood why. We were caught out in the open while artillery and mortars rained in on the tanks, shot to pieces from the rear side of Hill Nan and the front side of Hill 60; two tanks were knocked out and the third one ran and they had to smoke the draw to get us in. One of the riflemen didn't get back at all, and we never found his body, even after we took the ground. We dragged another in by his belt and he was dead.

In the knobs like Nan and 60 and "Sugar Loaf" (there were two of them) only one company could attack at a time; G, E and F took their turns, and the major and the lieutenant and I went on every one of the company attacks. The bitterest fighting I saw in the war was on "Sugar Loaf," with E Company—where we hit the hill, got knocked back, hit it again and held, even though not a man could get his head above ground and a husky company runner who tried got shot through the head. But, shoot, stab and burn, the riflemen took the knobs and we ran around the edge of the main ridge along a railroad embankment and came up just below the Shuri ridge.

Then we rested. We had taken a lot of real estate, but we had lost a lot of men. We had Hill Nan and Hill 60, and the western end of Dekeshi, and all the high ground from the west side of Wana Ridge to the sea; but Murph had been hit and Chief had been hit and Jim and Ralph and Sam had been hit. Larry, the old OP runner from Peleliu, had been hit worst of all.

The First Marine Regiment went into a rest area and new men were pumped into the companies to replace the old men who were casualties. At least, the new men replaced the old men on the platoon rosters; they did not replace them in the minds and hearts of their friends who were left. For two days I lay on my blankets back in the rest area, afraid to visit the other outfits to get the news. I heard that Bart, over in the First Battalion, had been hit and I was afraid to inquire about the others. Tony tried to cheer me but I was bad company until the evening he came around with Lieutenant Mac. Mac and I talked through one whole night. I can't remember what he said, but next morning, when orders came to move up to Dekeshi for an assault on Shuri itself, I was ready. Mac's old jokes had fixed me fine.

The First Regiment was swung inland to the ridge above Dekeshi Village. Across a broad valley was Wana; and just behind it, Shuri itself. The Seventh Marines had fought bitterly for Dekeshi; no topsoil or trees were left there and the earth had been blasted down to powdery rock. Below the lip of the ridge the town of Dekeshi was a shambles of stone and thatch, where roofs and walls had been. There the companies of the First Marines formed up to attack across the valley to Wana. On Dekeshi we did our observing from behind jagged coral spires that were like the peaks and gables of an old house. We stared out at Wana Ridge and Shuri.

On Wana Ridge, across the valley which was broad and sloped up, the artillery preparation had been laid on, and shellbursts rippled across the skyline and smoke was backwashed down into the valley. As the attack went out, the major ordered me to cross behind the fronts of the companies and make contact with the Army Infantry companies on our left flank.

I moved down through the scrambled stones and wall panels of the village just as our line swung out across the valley and moved forward in a long sweep of running riflemen. While it lasted, it was something worth watching. It was the kind of open and extended attack that appears in the movies but which is rarely seen in actual combat. For the few minutes that it moved ahead it was exciting to see. But suddenly it all stopped, and the line went down as some men were hit and the rest of them had to "hit the deck" to protect themselves against the fire from Shuri.

The Japanese poured it down from Shuri. The valley flamed orange with shellbursts. Where there had been hundreds of men running forward, there was no longer any sign of human life—only the inhuman flames belched high by heavy artillery and smaller orange bursts from mortar blasts, and the winking, blinking machine-gun tracers which streaked through the smoke.

I went on toward the Army's Seventy-seventh Division lines, ducking into holes and creeping along walls as the fire came back from Shuri.

I cut into the Seventy-seventh Division area near a small peak which broke the continuity of their line with that of the First Marines. Army riflemen were moving around the peak, and some were squatting in the road just behind it. Small-arms fire was very heavy there and nobody walked erect. A rifleman told me they had moved into the area early that morning and were trying to turn the corner of the small peak. He did not have to tell me why they were held up. Wounded streamed by—some carried; some hobbling; some running and frantic; some crawling or supported upright between two buddies.

"It gets bad right there," he said, pointing to the edge of the peak about twenty-five yards ahead. "Minute we turn the corner we get hit, heavy. We're pinned down."

"You've got to turn that corner," I told him. The Marines are going through the main valley."

"You better tell that to an officer," he said. "I just lug a rifle here." He was a big, strong-looking man and didn't seem either frightened or anxious to move ahead. He sat rock-solid against the hillside, ready to do what he had to do and no more.

I crept ahead and found the company commander, just back from the edge of the hill. I told him my story and he scarcely looked at me, except to make sure I had no rank. Then he turned back to his own problem. When I pressed him he got annoyed and snapped: "We're doing what we can, and we don't need any Marines crying on our necks." His hand swept around, indicating all the men crouched low in their holes. "You want to lead a charge?" he asked. "Those are bullets humming, fellah!"

I started back toward the Marine lines. When I came to the gap at the Army-Marine boundary I had to crawl. The Japanese were dumping a heavy load of shellfire on the gap. They didn't hit much, because there were no troops there. I crawled through the fire. I wasn't afraid of it any more, as long as I could keep moving and didn't have to lie under it too long. Shellfire was getting to be familiar, and familiarity was breeding contempt, or at least carelessness.

When I had reported, the colonel said to the major, "You'd better go out there, Major, and see what you can do to persuade them to move. The Japs are pouring it onto us from that hump."

When the Major and I got back to the Army lines the captain took us out to show us the situation on the hill. To get out there we had to crawl along a narrow trench. It was the only cover. Overhead the fire criss-crossed from every side.

"I got a platoon beyond that hill," the lieutenant in charge explained. He didn't get up in the ditch to point it out. "But that platoon can't get its head up. It's pinned flat."

The captain did raise himself up so he could peer over the edge of the trench. The major did the same thing. "See that hill," the captain said. "Look at the back side of it!" I looked over the top of the trench. The back side of the hump was studded with caves and gun positions. I didn't see any sign of the lieutenants' platoon. They were keeping low and I didn't blame them. It was an impossible position to hold.

We had to crawl backwards out of the trench. There wasn't enough depth to turn around in. "Tanks are on their way," the captain told us. "Once we can give those gun positions a mouthful of steam we can move on by. But until then I'm not moving up a foot."

The major didn't argue. He sent me back to report to the colonel. I started down the road. If I had to circle the line I was going to do it from far back.

I was thinking of this as I walked along, upright. This time my odds had run out. I suppose a mortarburst hit me—I never heard it or saw the flash. I came to on the roadside, with my ears ringing and my leg sticky with blood. I felt no pain, only the shock and surprise that comes with a wound. Nobody ever really expects to be hit and it comes as a bad surprise when it happens.

For a moment I didn't want to look to see how bad the wound was. I said a prayer and then I rolled over on my side and pulled up my trouser-leg. There were five punctures in my right leg; four of them were oozing but the fifth was bleeding heavily. I was frightened and I began to yell and, as I did, mortar fire dropped in on the road and drowned the noise I made. I began to crawl back along the roadside. I stopped once and used my battle dressing on the deep wound, but it didn't help much, and before I had gone far it was soaked and dripping through. I crawled until I tumbled into a hole where two Army medics were working over a wounded man.

"I'm hit," I told them. I had started out frightened. Now I was terrified.

"Bad?"

"I think it's bad. It's bleeding a lot."

"Wait a minute," the medic said. He finished working on the wounded man and came over and knelt beside me. He squeezed and pressed in around the wound. "It's not bad," he said. "I'll get that bleeding stopped."

As soon as the medic spoke, the fear left me. I

relaxed and lit a cigarette. The worst part of a wound is being alone and not knowing how bad it is. Once you reach a medical man it becomes his problem and the fear disappears. He stopped the bleeding and patched the small punctures. "Any pain?" he asked me. "I mean I know you were scared, but did it hurt?"

"No," I had to admit. "It didn't hurt."

"It's probably clean." He stood up and walked out to the road. The mortar fire had lifted. "I'd better send you back to an evac hospital just the same. There might be something in that hole that has to come out. . . . Hey!" He was calling to two army riflemen who were walking back along the road. "Help this guy back to the pick-up station."

To me he said, "Keep the weight off so you don't bust out bleeding again. Lean on them and drag the bad leg." He tied a tag on me and patted me as though I were a side of beef ready for the meat cutter. The two riflemen got their shoulders under my arms and we straggled off down the road.

"What happened?" one of them asked. He didn't really care, but it was the standard question asked of a wounded man.

"I got some mortar fragments in my leg."

"You're lucky. How come you got that funny-looking helmet?"

"I'm a Marine."

He twisted his face and grinned at me. "I'm surprised. I thought you guys cut the leg off and grew a new one when this happened."

"I don't feel so funny," I told him.

"Yeah," his partner said. "Just shut up and help the guy, willya?"

"I was only kidding," he said. "Trying to cheer up the wounded heroes."

"Just shut up," his partner said. "You got a big mouth and a small head."

At the pick-up station they put me in a small jeep ambulance. It had rained in the night and it began to rain again, and the jeep slid all over the road, going in from the line. I tried to find room in the ambulance to stretch out my leg and rest it. It was aching.

There were two men on stretchers in the jeep, and there was no leg room. Both of the wounded soldiers seemed to be hurt bad. One of the men groaned as the jeep bumped and slithered on the mud. The other man was silent. When they unloaded them at the evac hospital the quiet one was dead and the groaning one was groaning worse. A medic told him to shut up and a woman nurse went into a rage at the medic. The nurse looked at my ticket and then got two aides to help me over to a bench.

When they brought me into a surgical tent, a tired-eyed doctor was standing there smoking. While he looked at my wound, he let the smoke curl up into his eyes. It made my own eyes water just to watch him, but he ignored the irritation of the smoke in his eyes. He began to pinch and knead the flesh of the calf of my leg and I grunted from the pain. He paid no more attention to my grunts than to the smoke in his eyes.

"You got out of it easy," he said. "I think it's clean except for one small splinter of shrapnel."

"In the big hole?" I asked.

"That's not a big hole. You should see some of them. No, not in that one. That was just a sideswipe. The splinter is in one of the small punctures. I'll get it."

I saw him reach for a straight steel instrument and I jumped off the edge of the cot. A nurse came into the room behind me. I could smell scent, but I didn't turn to look at her. The doctor said to her, "Just a little weight on his shoulders and hold him in one place. He seems jumpy."

The nurse put two large and beautifully clean hands on my shoulders and pressed me back down on the cot. The doctor began to use the steel probe. I strained against the hands. They were strong. From the corner of my eye I saw a wisp of blond hair which came loose from her cap and brushed my forehead. The perfumed soap she used was the nicest thing I had smelled for months. I was surprised when the doctor said, "Got it! This really is your lucky day, young man. In a few days you'll be ready to get back there, good as new."

"What's lucky about that, Doc?"

The nurse said, "I thought Marines were unhappy when they weren't out fighting."

"I'm exceptional," I told her. "I'm a coward. If you have any odd jobs, I'd be glad to stay back here and work for my room and board."

The doctor lit another cigarette from the stub of the last one. He never took them out of his mouth but puffed them down to the lip-line. "I wish they were all as easy as you," he said. "Take him away, nurse. I'll send the bill out at the end of the month." He grinned around his cigarette.

"I hope I'm around to pay it, Doc. It will be a pleasure."

The nurse helped me out of the surgical tent and over to a ward tent. I wanted to talk to her but I couldn't think of anything to say. I asked her name and where she came from in the States. She told me. She asked me the same. I told her. She came from the Midwest and I came from the East. That didn't make much conversation. She asked me how it was up on the lines. I said, "Pretty bad." There wasn't much else to say. I had never been more anxious, and less able, to talk to anyone. I almost clutched her hand to keep her from leaving me. I didn't and she said, "You'll be fine here," and left the ward tent.

After she was gone I lay on my cot and I could think of a lot to say but when another nurse came in to ask me if I wanted a pill, all I said was, "No, thanks, no pill. I'll sleep fine. I've very tired." And I was. Before I went to sleep I thought about women. They were like some strange people from another country. I didn't know their language any longer, but it was fine to have them around. It made me feel safer. I slept.

They discharged me from the hospital the next afternoon and gave me an ambulance ride up to the Marine medical tents where they treated the slightly wounded and gave emergency aid to the badly injured. The tents couldn't have been far behind the lines, because there was heavy artillery slamming away nearby. It was raining when they dropped me off, and I stood leaning against the side of an ambulance looking at the medical tents. They were surrounded by a sea of mud and inside they looked damp and dark and cheerless. I was back in a man's world again. Under the rolled-up sides I saw a clutter of equipment and men. As I turned around and hobbled back toward the highway, a jeep stopped. In the jeep were a Marine colonel and a sergeant.

"Going back up to the lines, son?" the colonel asked me.

I stood there a minute. "Yes, sir," I finally said. I still had my rifle. I had carried it all the way back to the hospital in the ambulance.

"Hop in," the colonel said. I stowed my rifle in back and climbed into the jeep. "Hit?" the colonel asked me. He probably had seen me limping.

"Just in the leg. There was no sense hanging around back there."

He shook his head in admiration. "Attaboy," he said. "The quicker we get in there, the quicker we get it done and get out. Right?"

I nodded and thought: Yeah, if we get out at all.

"I'd like to have a regiment of kids like this," the colonel told the sergeant.

The sergeant didn't say anything. He probably knew I was a phony of some kind. The jeep was open and it began to rain harder. The colonel and the sergeant put on ponchos. I sat there in my dungaree jacket, wet and miserable. The worst thing was that my leg didn't even hurt. It was healing and my chance for a vacation from the lines was gone. The colonel was a big and cheerful man. He said, "You won't have to be out there much longer, son."

It only takes a second to get hit good, I thought.

"We're going to bust right through them," the colonel said.

So are we, I thought.

"Once this rain stops, we'll . . ."

This rain will never stop, I thought.

The rain didn't stop. It came down harder each day and the trails and roads were buried in the mud that slipped and melted from the hills. The hills were glaciers of mud and they discharged their ooze down into the valleys. When the ground was ripped by shellfire it bled mud. It was a full day's work to walk the length of the line and back, and the major and I had a battalion front to cover. The troops were stalled up on Wana, and they were isolated from the rear by a sea of mud in the valley. When shells hit, the mud and slime shot high in that valley and to walk through it was impossible. Many nights I stayed out on the line because I didn't have the strength to walk back. My blanket was soaked and stank of mildew; my rifle rusted, even with a daily oiling. Water dripped into every meal and spoiled every cigarette. I didn't have the satisfaction of feeling sorry for myself, because for the riflemen and machine-gunners it was far worse.

I threw away my soggy blanket because it was too heavy to carry. I slept under my poncho and spent the nights in clammy misery. I was running a constant and chronic fever, especially at night. I stopped eating. I could not hold down coffee, and all my nourishment came from mushing chocolate bars up in hot water in a canteen cup. On the line, at that time, we knew that almost any wound meant certain death. It would be nearly impossible to get a man back through the mud in the valley. The thought of dying in the mud was a terrible one that haunted my dreams. And there was nothing in the war situation to offer any interest. We weren't taking any ground. We weren't giving any up. We were fighting a war of attrition, and the Marines did this kind of fighting badly. Supply was very bad. While the Army ate hot food, we had cold rations and silly speeches.

I was coming in from the lines to the Battalion Command Post, slipping down the back of Dekeshi Ridge toward the muddy horseshoe where Headquarters had been set up. I had been feeling dizzy and I was running a temperature and, though the wound on my leg had healed, my knee had stiffened up from the way I had limped and favored my leg. I started to fall and I tried to balance myself with my rifle. When it slipped I went skidding down the hill on my face. When I came to a stop I couldn't get up, and so I lay there. It was raining but it seemed to me that it had been raining ever since I was born. I lay in the rain without trying to cover my face.

When I came to, two wiremen were trying to lift me. I was so filthy and slippery with mud that they couldn't get a grip on me. Finally, one of them boosted me up and took me down the hill in a fireman's carry.

I don't remember the ride back in the ambulance. I was unconscious and a stretcher case when they brought me into the Marine medical tents back near the artillery. I remember a stab in the arm as they put in glucose intravenously. I remember getting some quinine; and then I was on my old malaria elevator, lurching up and down and never stopping. I burned and shook my way from half-consciousness to full coma and back again.

One of the Combat Intelligence scouts was also back there with malaria. He had finished the worst of his attacks when I came in and he nursed me and fed me.

After two days I was all right and they loaded us on a big, open truck to go back to the lines. The truck driver got lost and took us back from the lines instead of forward. When nightfall came, we were farther back than the medical tents. We unloaded from the truck and debated what to do. I was sitting between a platoon sergeant named Ray and a rifleman called "Highpockets."

"What'll we do?" Highpockets asked. "I'm not going to walk back to those lines, that's for sure."

"We couldn't do it anyway," Ray said. "I don't even know the way. Oh, for some warm chow and a bed!"

"I know where we can get both," I said. I told them about the evac hospital I had been in. I remembered the number.

"That's for us," Ray decided. "Let's go before somebody else gets the idea."

We went out to the highway and flagged down a weapons carrier going to the rear. I gave him the name of the evacuation hospital and the driver took us right to the gate. I remembered the name of the nurse who had held me down and I went around to her ward to see her. They said she wasn't on duty but she would look in at the end of the movie. We sat down on a cot and waited. I fell asleep, then I felt someone shaking me—and it was the nurse.

"What on earth are you doing here?" she asked me.

I explained to her what had happened. She was doubtful. "I don't know. We could all get into a lot of trouble for this. You're supposed to be with your units or have evacuation tickets. Have you been wandering around like this since we sent you up?"

"No. I went back up the next day. But I came down with malaria and the after-effects of the wound. We're not deserters. All we want is some hot food and a dry bed for one night. We started up this afternoon, but the truck driver got lost."

The nurse walked over to the entry way of the ward tent and stood looking out into the dark. An ambulance from the lines swung in off the highway; its lights showed a muddy waste of yard and two stretcher-bearers running forward against the slanting rain in the receiving area. The tires sucked and slapped across the area, and in the darkness someone called: "Four, and all bad ones."

The nurse said, "It must be terrible up there to-night." She turned back to us. "Well, we've got a few empty cots over in that other ward tent." As we started out of the tent with her, she said, "Are those the only shoes you have?"

My boots had rotted out through the toes from the rain and mud. I had very small feet and I hadn't been able to get another pair. I explained that to her. "I'll give you my boots," she said. "They ought to fit you. But tomorrow, for heaven's sake, go back before you get us all in trouble."

She got us a bed, clean and out of the rain. She got us hot food from the galley. I couldn't eat much of it because my stomach had shrunk, but it was nice to play with hot food and waste it if we wanted to. I almost fell asleep into my tray.

In the morning she brought over her boots and gave them to me and they did fit. "We'll go on up now," I told her. "Thank you for everything. I don't think I could have gone up there last night. Today, I can."

"I know. Some days I don't think I can ever walk into the bad wards again. I run off duty and get into my cot and cry and cry. And then afterwards it changes and I go back."

"We can't cry," Highpockets told her. He fished his rifle out from under his cot and slung it. He was a miserable-looking Marine, even in rest area; in combat he looked like an armed scarecrow: bony, lank and ragged.

"I know you can't cry," she said. "I'm glad you came to me. I hope I'll see you next time in a better place than this."

"We'll see you when the war is over, in Nebraska," I said. "What did you say the name of that town was?"

She told me.

"O. K. We'll see you there."

Before we left the hospital she got us sandwiches and new, dry blankets. She was the only woman to whom I talked directly all the time I was in the Pacific. She was the best of her kind. I had forgotten that there were such creatures as women and that they could show tender kindness that was impossible even from the best of men.

Riding up to the lines on a truck, we talked of the nurse. Highpockets decided that when the campaign was over he was going to draw his pay and send her the best present he could buy. I told them that I planned to write to her. I meant it; but in the mud and rain of the days which followed, the paper with her name and address on it got ruined and finally lost. I never wrote to her and I doubt that Highpockets ever sent her any present.

We came back to the line. It was on Wana Ridge, right where we had left it a few days before. There was one bad day and night and then all went quiet out in front of the line. The next day we crossed a deep gully, went through high piles of stone and rubble, and climbed the hill into Shuri.

All that was standing was a church with a cross on it. Some said it was a sign from God, and others pointed out that the church was masked from direct artillery fire by a fold in the hill. Whatever the case, it was good to see. The Japanese main line of defense on the Naha–Shuri side had cracked and their army was in full retreat toward the southern end of the island.

13

LAST STAND ON THE YUZA DAKE

On the hills near the Yuza Dake escarpment, the Japanese turned to make their last stand, and the Marines, each man walking, each man carrying a weapon, stumbled on toward them, along a road that had no end ahead in the gray rain, no bottom below in the mire and no side boundaries, as hills and roads and rivers oozed together in one slimy, clutching horror of mud. One rifleman lost his boot in the mud and almost lost his fingers as men in the file came on through the muck and marched over his hand. The country seemed to have been chewed up and spat out by some sloppy giant.

In the mud were Japanese dead, abandoned and burned trucks, ruined artillery pieces and caissons and the offal of an army that had been broken in war but was not as yet smashed in spirit. The Japanese left nothing of value behind, scared, miserable and helpless though they must have felt as the diving, rocketing planes and naval gunfire dogged every step of their retreat. They still took the trouble to booby-trap the dead.

Tony and I were sent out through the low hills along the road to collect the documents of Japanese dead and send them back to Intelligence. We approached our dead with caution, circling the corpse, kneeling down to peer under it, and turning it over with a rifle butt. We had lost a man when a corpse blew up in his face.

We had got too far off the road and into the hills, and we were swinging back when Tony waved toward a gully.

From the rim we saw the bloated hump of a Japanese corpse. The Japanese had been hit with fifty-caliber machine gun fire from a strafing plane and he had dragged himself a long way from the road. His snakelike trail had not yet been erased by the rain and Tony had spotted it. We could see as we approached that he had not been mined. I flipped him over and began to cut the sodden pockets off his tunic.

"I feel like a grave robber," Tony said.

I handed Tony a soggy wallet stuffed with papers. We spread a poncho on the ground and began to sort through the papers—the biggest lump of them were pictures and letters. There was a picture of a dignified old Japanese gentleman.

"Father," Tony said.

There was a picture of a broad-faced lady still with jet-black hair. "Mother," Tony said.

There was a younger woman in full kimono and obi. "Wife or sweetheart," Tony said.

There was a picture of a chubby, black-eyed boy. "Kid," Tony said. "Then it must have been wife—the young one, I mean. Handsome kid, isn't he?"

At that moment, for the first time in the war, I felt pity for the enemy. On Peleliu we had seen few enemy dead. They had been dragged into caves by their mates or sealed in bunkers by our demolitionists. On Okinawa I had seen hundreds of dead, but I felt nothing toward them until we searched that Japanese in the gully and found the pictures of his wife and child. Then I realized that we were killing other humans who fathered children and had parents who loved them, just as we had.

I turned away from the corpse and busied myself with the letters. There were two packets, each tied with different colored ribbon. I read no Japanese but I knew one packet came from the old man or woman and the other from the young woman. I put those aside along with a belt of a thousand stitches—probably made by the mother to bring her son luck—a small Rising Sun flag and a military emblem on a black ribbon chain. There was also a wood carving, perhaps a toy for the black-eyed child. I put that aside.

"Probably for his kid," Tony said. "He musta made it himself."

"All right," I said, "it was for his kid. I didn't start this war."

There was a black book—an account book or diary. I put that in the pile for Intelligence. There was the torn fragment of a situational map. I put that in the pile. There were documents with Japanese numbers, probably ration statements or supply reports. They went into the pile. There was a small paper-bound book with what appeared to be Japanese verse. I debated and finally put it in the Intelligence pile. Later, a Japanese translator at Division told me that the book was full of short verses, about butterflies and hummingbirds and flowers, that the officer had written himself, perhaps to send to his wife. They called them *Hai Kai* or something like that.

The translator said, "He was a pretty good poet, that Jap."

That night both Tony and I asked to get off the Intelligence detail, but they wouldn't let us. Somebody had to do it and we weren't any more tender than anybody else. From that day in the rain I never again hated the Japanese. I just wished that the war would end so we could stop killing each other.

My memory of the move down the road toward the Yuza Dake is filled with scenes of mud, destroyed equipment and dead Japanese. We had the Japanese wounded and close to death, and we were closing in for the kill in what would be the last land battle of World War II.

Moving through the waste we began, after a day or two, to run against the forward positions of what remained of the Japanese army. At first there were only a few snipers harassing our forward patrols by making them dive into the mud. Then there were minor strong points, hills or ravines defended by five- or six-man squads.

As we moved through the hills below the Yuza Dake and Kunishi Ridge, Japanese artillery began to come down on us again. The fire was far lighter than it had been near Shuri, because the Japanese had already lost most of their

artillery. Still the fire held us up. There was a big fight on
a hill near Yuza and another fight for a hill near Ozato.
When we had those hills, we could look south toward
rising, open country which rolled on up to the foot of the
escarpment. The major pointed toward Kunishi Ridge and
the escarpment.

"That's where they'll stand with what force they have."
As we watched, men and tanks went out along the one
road that cut through the center of the valley. Artillery fire
came down and the men and tanks turned back. "This is
the last big one," the major said. "But it could be bad.
There is no cover in that valley."

Artillery fired TOT (Time on Target) into the ridge.
The 105's, the 155's, the naval guns and the 75's on tanks
dug in behind our hill, struck with one long roar at the
ridge, but no men could get across the valley. A second air
strike was called down and this time two of the planes lost
the target and strafed far behind the Marine lines. In one
day, early on Okinawa, our battalion was hit by our own
rocket run, strafed by our own planes, shelled by our own
artillery and smashed by our own naval guns. Such mistakes were inevitable, just as men where shot by their own
mates on the lines. The wonder of it was that we lost so
few men by mistakes.

105 mm Howitzer

As we turned back down from the hill at nightfall, the major said: "We'll never take the hill in a daylight assault without losing a lot of men. We may see some night work."

Back in the higher echelons, the generals had reached the same conclusion. "Take Kunishi with a night assault," was the order. The Marines were not throwing away any more men than was necessary to deal out the deathblow. The night assault was the right order; or at least it seemed to be, to officers and men.

The companies assembled at the place where the road up the valley cut between two hills. And though the move was made in total darkness, two companies were deployed to the right of the road and they waited there in silence while an occasional flare popped overhead and artillery droned over toward the ridge. The major and I waited in a hole behind the commander of one of the assault companies.

In the darkness the commander quietly assigned the lead-off platoons and told the lieutenants what little was known of the ground out ahead. There was nothing more to do then but wait for the word to move ahead. Men talked quietly or stared ahead into the alternating green and black of the night. A machine-gun section picked up its tools with a clatter and prepared to move out to a position where they could give covering fire up the first slope. If they saw nothing, they were ordered not to fire at all. One of them grumbled, "I ain't never heard of a night attack before. What a screwy thing! How do we know what we're firing at?"

"Don't fire unless you're told to," someone growled at him. "Just shut your fat trap and sit behind your gun and do what you're told."

"Someone comes at me in the dark," the machine-gunner said, "I'm gonna fire. I'm gonna ride this gun. That's all I got going for me out there."

One of the officers of the rifle platoon said, "Shut up and move out and wait for the word before you do anything." The machine-gunners moved out, grumbling.

"What time you figure we'll move, Major?" the company commander asked.

"Should be pretty soon now. They want to make it

late enough so some of them will be sleeping out there. But it will be well before dawn. It will take about fifteen or twenty minutes for the men to get up on the ridge—if all goes well!"

"I think it will take more than that. The ground is pretty broken."

"Maybe it will at that. We're allowing more than an hour for them to get across."

A rifleman began to whistle through his teeth, softly. He was shushed.

Somebody said, "Boy, I'm nervous!"

Somebody else said: "Who isn't?"

"It's just the waiting to jump off that gets you," the company commander told them. "But I wish they'd knock off those flares. What do we need them for?"

"It's the Army," the major said. "They may be afraid of a counterattack."

"The Japs won't attack," the company commander said. "Why should they? They got all the high ground there is."

"I wish they'd hurry up," a company runner muttered. "I'd like to see what we're going to hit out there."

"You'll know soon enough."

"Those flares are still going up," the company commander said to his radioman. "Get Battalion and tell them to knock off the illumination." There was the low mutter of the radioman talking into his set. Off to the left a brisk fire fight flared up on a hillside. Machine-gun tracers plunged out into the dark of the valley and died like lost meteorites; mortars burst in dull orange and then the sound of their *harrumpf* followed. Company illumination went up and there were shouts.

"Some Jap maybe snored in his sleep," a scout muttered behind me. "For that, they shoot up the whole area and wake up the Japs."

"How's our liaison with the Army?" the company commander asked the major. "Do we have good contact?"

"I hope so," the major answered. "I sure hope so. They could murder us if we haven't."

There was a call coming in from Battalion Headquarters. Both the major and the company commander spoke.

When he had finished talking on the radio, the company commander said: "That was the word. First platoon, let's move out—softly."

I started forward with the first platoon. We had taken no more than fifty careful paces when a flare burst overhead. I crouched down. "Those crazy fools," the platoon leader snarled. "Tell the skipper I'm not moving until they get control of that illumination."

We all crouched down in the holes. The man beside me was shaking so much that his gear rattled. I was terrified. The company commander came forward and talked to the lieutenant. We started to move forward again. As I walked I counted; not that the number of paces meant anything—I counted to control my fear. It was better than screaming aloud. We couldn't afford to make any sound.

Near me, a man muttered: "It will be daylight soon." As though no one heard him, he repeated the same words: "It will be daylight soon." When nobody answered him, he said for the third time: "It will be daylight soon."

"Shut up!" Somebody had at last answered him. He was quiet, apparently satisfied. All around in the darkness riflemen were shuffling forward. Directly ahead of me was a BAR man. I had already run against his weapon in the darkness. The ground was broken and it was hard to walk quietly. Someone tripped and sprawled and his rifle clanked. He was cursed, softly.

Off ahead came a high, weird call that made everyone stop.

"Some lousy bird or something," a voice said.

We were moving through Japanese-held positions, but I was only occasionally aware of the danger around us in the dark. In the blackness only the loom of the hills showed. We were moving away from the road and the ground was rising as we went. Off to the left a fire burned on a hillside. I wished I were there, wherever it was. We walked on into the dark.

Suddenly a flare burst. Enormous light showered down on us, and we were too startled to realize what had happened until we had taken a pace or two more. The whole line of men was outlined in bright green light. A Japanese rifle popped. Then a Nambu ripped open the darkness, off beyond the circle of light from the flare. We dived for what cover there was.

Somebody yelled: "Run for that hill there!"

I ran for a hulking shadow that I thought was the hill. A second flare burst. A BAR opened up and the surprise attack on Kunishi was over. I fell down into a gully that was filled with running men. I didn't know whether they were Japanese or Americans. I stayed low and crawled along the gully until I came to a branching ditch. I followed that for a while and then lay down.

The firing died off. Men were still moving and it was never quiet again. I had crawled along the ditch, trying to remember how to get out and back toward the road. I couldn't. I was lost. Somewhere, heavy artillery began to land. It wasn't near where I was, and the ditch seemed as safe a place as any to be. I didn't want to crawl out behind Japanese lines. Since I had no plan, I lay down in the ditch and waited. If I moved ahead, the Japanese would have me. If I moved back, the reserve platoon might shoot me. Over my shoulder I could see that the sky was beginning to show light above where I thought the Army lines were. I watched as the sky peeped open in a long, almond-shaped slit, like an Oriental eye. I took that to be a bad sign.

I lay in the ditch as dawn came and the fire whispered across the gully. I still had no notion which way was back. I drank some water and worked myself lower into the bottom of the ditch. When full light came, I would know whether or not I was lying under the rifle sights of a Japanese sniper. As the sun came up higher, I managed to get into motion and crawled along the ditch toward what I judged was the north.

I was moving on my stomach and using my elbows. My legs felt numb and useless, but I dragged them along anyway. When I came to the end of the ditch, I found a rock outcropping. There the first sniper of the day found me. He put a ringing shot in over my neck. I felt the sting of the rock fragments. The shot took the paralysis out of my legs. I crouched and then dashed for another rock across the gully. The sniper kicked up rock dust behind me and got one more in, close, when I stopped. I took a deep breath and turned the corner. Nobody fired and I had half a mountain between me and the sniper.

I drove ahead under fire and came to a place where there was a long ridge of rock with one gap in the middle of it. I crawled out to the gap. On the other side was the reserve platoon. They were ducking across, one at a time. At least, that was what they were trying to do. One of them lay out in the gap, hit by a sniper who had it under fire. When they saw me, someone yelled and waved and said: "Lay it onto that rock up there." I could see where he pointed. The sniper was up behind a rock. I opened fire on the rock and two of the reserve platoon came dashing across. They put BAR fire on the rock, and then the rest of the platoon came across. I ran back the other way.

I went to where the attack had jumped off and asked for the major. He had gone back up to the Observation Post, on the hill. I went up there and joined him and tried to sleep, but the flies and heat were too bad.

In the afternoon the men out on the lower slope of the ridge were stranded. They couldn't get their wounded back, or reinforcements up. One company had tried to move up and been knocked back. Reports said "Medium to heavy casualties with a lot of men isolated and hit."

The major called me to him late in the afternoon. "Can we move stretcher-bearers up on the hill?" he asked. "The kids are catching it something awful. They're pulling some out in tanks, but there are more than the tanks can handle."

"There is one bad place," I said. "If they can get by there, they might go all the way." I was thinking of the unprotected gap in the low ridge. "I know the place from this morning."

"See if you can get 'em out there," the major told me. "They need help bad on the hill."

I got out to the gap with the stretcher teams, but

things were worse: instead of one rifleman, the Japanese
had moved in machine-gun-and-mortar cover. We started
out twice, and were driven back when bearers were hit. It
seemed better to send the stretcher-bearers out in the
tanks, along with water and supplies. some of the stretcher-
bearers said they would try to make a run through the
open field. I don't know how many of them made it, but
three teams went up in the tanks. I went back.

When night came, a second company was moved up
across the open ground to the ridge. I went out with them
and we got into a confused fire-fight and I was pinned
down for two hours or more. When I crawled back to the
Observation Post I was sent out again with a jeep ambulance to pick up the wounded. I don't even remember how
we got out there or back. I was walking in my sleep by
that time. When I came in, I collapsed by the roadside
and slept until dawn.

I woke on what was to be our last day of combat. Up
on the hill men were cracking from the heat and the
strain, and the only way up and back was with tanks.
Every gully and ridge was swept with fire, and the Japanese
had encircled the men on the ridge. I spent all morning
trying to get up on the ridge, and all afternoon trying to
come in. In one gully I was pinned down so long I actually
fell asleep. It wasn't that I had grown contemptuous of
danger. I was suffering from overpowering fatigue that
made everything that happened a blur.

When I came in at nightfall, the major said: "I got
good news. They're going to pull the kids out tonight."

Just after dark I started into the ridges with two
guides that the company had sent out by tank in the
afternoon. Flares popped as we moved up toward the
hills, but we were never under fire. We found the first
company commander and gave him the news:

"You're going out."

"Thank God. Can we get out?"

"You can get out. We just came in."

"Pass the word to the platoons. We're going out."

The men came out along the road and between the last hills, and when they were through the gap there was a sigh of relief all along the column. We were in the clear. I sat down on an ammunition box just inside the gap and lit a cigarette. I was falling off the box with sleepiness.

As the men in the last company came down the road and through the gap, the commander saw me and asked: "Where's the colonel?"

I showed the company commander where he could find the colonel and the Command Post. The commander thanked me and said, "You missed something out on that hill."

I didn't say anything. That was my last duty in combat: showing the commander how to find the colonel. I sat down on the ammunition box again and changed out my rotted socks. I was done with the war.

The Japanese generals were about done with the war, too, but they ended it with more impressive symbolism than a change of socks.

The History of the First Marine Division reports the account of a captured Japanese soldier who witnessed the final scene—the suicide of General Ushijima, Commander of Japanese forces on Okinawa.

Four o'clock, the final hour of *hari-kiri*; the Commanding General, dressed in full field uniform, and the Chief of Staff in a white kimono, appear. . . . The Chief of Staff says, as he leaves the cave first:

"Well, Commanding General Ushijima, as the way may be dark, I, Cho, will lead the way."

The Commanding General replies, "Please do so, and I'll take along my fan since it is getting warm." Saying this, he picks up his Okinawa-made fan and walks out, quietly fanning himself. . . .

The moon, which has been shining until now, sinks below the waves of the western sea. Dawn has not yet arrived and, at 0410, the generals appear at the mouth of the cave. The American forces are only three meters away.

A sheet of white cloth is placed on a quilt. . . . The

Commanding General and the Chief of Staff sit down on the quilt, bow in reverence to the eastern sky, and Adjutant J—— respectfully presents his sword. . . .

At this time several grenades were hurled near this solemn scene by the enemy troops, who observed movements taking place beneath them. A simultaneous shout and a flash of a sword, then another repeated shout and a flash, and both generals had nobly accomplished their last duty to their Emperor. . . .

Things end differently for different men.